The
Money Tree

Other titles by Chris Guillebeau

Side Hustle
The Happiness of Pursuit
The $100 Startup
The Art of Non-Conformity

The

Money Tree

A Story About Finding the
Fortune in Your Own Backyard

Chris Guillebeau

Portfolio / Penguin

Portfolio / Penguin
An imprint of Penguin Random House LLC
penguinrandomhouse.com

Most Portfolio books are available at a discount when purchased in quantity for sales
promotions or corporate use. Special editions, which include personalized covers, excerpts,
and corporate imprints, can be created when purchased in large quantities. For more
information, please call (212) 572-2232 or e-mail specialmarkets@penguinrandomhouse
.com. Your local bookstore can also assist with discounted bulk purchases using the
Penguin Random House corporate Business-to-Business program. For assistance
in locating a participating retailer, e-mail B2B@penguinrandomhouse.com.

ISBN 9780593188712 (hardcover)
ISBN 9780593188729 (ebook)

Printed in the United States of America
1   3   5   7   9   10   8   6   4   2

Book design by Alexis Farabaugh

The
Money Tree

Act I

1.

"Jake, are you there? Did we lose you?"

In his mind, Jake Aarons felt fully in control of his life. Not only had he stopped worrying about the highly disturbing emails he'd received right before the client meeting, but the problems they referred to didn't exist at all. He imagined a bright future with his girlfriend and a promising career at the agency.

But in the conference room where he sat, situated across from his boss and two seats away from the client who had just signed a major contract, he wasn't paying any attention at all. Even as he daydreamed about an alternate reality, he knew that the one he was suddenly facing was far less desirable. If only he could—

"Hey, Earth to Jake!"

"What? Oh . . . sorry. I was just gathering my thoughts."

He rewound the last few minutes in his mind, switching out of autopilot and willing himself to remember key details. Five people sat staring at him. First, his boss, Jan, who was leading the meeting and trying to get his attention. Next, two representatives of Avery Tech, the client that had hired them. A few seats farther over was Sloan, who carried the honorary title of Chief Asshole Officer. Sloan wasn't aware he held this high honor that Jake had conferred upon him. In his mind he saw himself as "Senior Consultant," despite the fact that their agency didn't organize its employees by rank. Finally, next to Sloan sat Preena, a much nicer colleague he'd come to consider a friend in the ten months he'd been working at Brightside.

And then there was Jake. What was he supposed to do again?

Now he remembered. He was supposed to present his group's ideas to help Avery Tech get out of its rut and go back to making money. Helping businesses make money is what marketers are supposed to do, after all.

He'd been distracted all morning, obsessing over some untimely news he'd received, but now it was time to rally. He cleared his throat and looked at the room, making eye contact with Jan and the client reps.

"So, uh, I thought we'd begin by looking at your social media accounts. I think you can do a lot more with them."

The group waited. *What more could they do with them, Jake?* Right. He needed to keep going.

"We can get into specifics as we go along, but I also wonder if you've thought about reaching out to some of your current customers for feedback. You know, just checking in to see if they have suggestions for improvement."

It was obvious he'd already lost them. That's what happens when you come to a pitch meeting with no ideas.

Jan cut in. "It's okay, Jake, I'll take over. Or actually, Sloan, did you have something to present?"

Sloan, Chief Asshole Officer, could always be counted on to land self-promotion points.

"Absolutely," he said, making sure he caught Jake's eye before continuing. "I've been doing a deep dive into your website analytics and noticed something really interesting. You guys sell memory chips and cards for computers, right?"

The client reps perked up.

"Well, it looks like most people who land on your site aren't actually searching for those things, at least not directly. They're searching for phrases like 'data storage' and 'computer processor.' Not only that, but if you separate the people who make purchases from those who just come in and leave, the people who arrive looking for data storage are 26 percent more likely to buy."

"That's really interesting," Client Rep One said, while Rep Two nodded and wrote something down.

"But here's the thing," Sloan said. "You don't really have a strategy to target people searching for data storage. I think that's where we should start. From there, we can look at retargeting, developing custom upsells, and otherwise extracting more value from all those visitors."

"Huh," Rep One said. "I don't think we knew anything about that."

The rest of the meeting proceeded from there. Jake went back into wallflower status, Jan ran the show, and Sloan made himself look good. Only Jake knew that this whole "deep dive into your website analytics" shtick actually came from Preena. She was going to present it when the toss came her way, but Sloan had pushed her aside in the lineup and run with it.

It was that kind of move that had led Jake to confer his honorary title on Sloan. He was always willing to go above and beyond, especially for his own benefit. Always the first to arrive in the morning and the last to leave at night, at least as long as everyone else knew about it.

Unfortunately, in an agency structure it was often those kinds of self-serving behaviors that ended up being rewarded.

As for Jake, he was frequently distracted, but not usually to the point of being such a space cadet. Especially when going into a meeting with clients, his boss, and his adversary, he tried to be prepared. But the fact was that he had a lot on his mind. Something had happened earlier that morning that threw off his balance: Jake had finally gotten around to reading his email from Tuesday.

Reading your Tuesday messages on Friday could be considered a power move for some people. Maybe if you were into that whole "don't check email in the morning" mindset, and decided to interpret it as "don't check email for several days at a time." Alternatively, it could end up getting you fired, or worse.

The first message that caught his attention had an ominous subject line:

Loan Collection Status

The message was from Midland Financial Services, which informed him that it had recently purchased Jake's student loan debt and was now seeking a payment schedule.

Eight years ago, Jake had discovered the miracle of student loans. "It's free money from the government!" his roommate said with the air of winning the lottery.

"Sounds amazing!" Jake said, and he signed the pages that would lead to a large deposit in his bank account, as well as a free toaster that he never unpacked from the box. He figured that he'd be able to afford to repay the money . . . someday. Wasn't that how it worked? Besides, it would be a *long* time before any payments became due.

It now seemed that this faraway day in the distant land of the future had arrived. Over the course of three years—he had a scholarship for much of his senior year—Jake had borrowed a total of $52,450.38. More than half of that had gone directly to California State University, Northridge. The other half had gone . . . somewhere. The loans stipulated that the money could only be spent on educational expenses, which by Jake's interpretation included rent, food, gas, a trip to Ireland with his older brother, Zach, and beer.

Midland was seeking repayment, with interest, on a schedule that called for the first payment of $805.14 to begin next month. The notice cheerfully informed him that a discount was available for making a larger payment.

Then Jake opened the next message. It was from Roland, the property manager who'd rented him his latest apartment. The apartment was the best place he'd ever lived, and it was greatly underpriced. Even Zach, who worked for a big startup in San Francisco, was impressed.

The message from Roland was titled:

Legal Notice re: Change in Rental Unit

Jake clicked on the link.

> Hi Jake,
> Hope you've been well. I'm sorry to bring bad news, but the owners of the condo you've been renting are planning to sell. They need the money to pay for their elderly grandmother's nursing home bills, and they want you out right away.
> By law, they have to give you 21 days' notice, and unfortunately they can't wait any longer than that. They also need to get in the unit to take photos, and once they publish the listing they'll have potential buyers coming through to see it. We'll need to plan some times for you to be out when that happens.

Again, sorry about the news. I know it's been a great spot
for you!

Roland Myers

Syndicate Leasing Group

Owing money he couldn't afford to pay was bad enough, but
not having a place to live was even worse. The message with
twenty-one days' notice was sent on Tuesday. It was now Friday
afternoon, which left . . . what, eighteen days at the outset?

Before his brilliant speech in the client presentation, he'd been
racking his brain trying to think of what to do. No obvious solutions presented themselves. Mostly, he just felt overwhelmed.

After the meeting, Jake slunk out to talk with his friend. "Preena! Why did you let Sloan do that to you?"

"What, steal my idea?"

"Yeah! I saw all those printouts on your desk. That whole thing
about diving into the analytics came from you."

"Well, yeah." She shrugged. "That wasn't cool. But what was I going
to do—start a fight in front of the client? He knew I wouldn't challenge him. Anyway, how are you? You seemed a little off in there."

Jake told her about the messages he'd finally gotten around to
reading.

"That's rough, Jake. I've got to get some client work done before
I go to my next meeting, but let's plan to talk about this more on
Monday."

"Of course." On the way back to his desk he passed by Sloan's
office. He imagined him sitting inside, reading *The Art of War* and

writing emails to management that recapped the client meeting with him in the starring role.

———

Working late that night and trying to build a better strategy for the client he'd disappointed, Jake didn't notice his phone flashing a reminder to leave for the most important appointment of his day: a dinner date with Maya, his girlfriend. When he heard a chime that signaled a text message from her, he looked down.

"Hey, Jake, this place is cute! I got here a few minutes early and snagged a table by the window. See you soon!"

Soon was a highly optimistic prediction, but Maya didn't know that.

"On my way!" he texted, grabbing his messenger bag and running for the door. In his mind he calculated the traffic: at least fifteen minutes, more like twenty at this time of day. Damn.

No big deal. It's only our six-month anniversary.

Just like it was only $50,000 he owed, with less than $3,000 in his savings account. Just like all he needed to do was find a way to start paying that off, at the same time he was finding a new place to live.

On his way out, Jan flagged him down. "Hey, Jake, can we talk for a minute?"

"Uh, sure. I'm just late to meet Maya . . ."

"I'll be quick. I'm a little concerned about you. With the merger coming up, management is going to be making some hard decisions."

It wasn't really a merger, though everyone called it that. Brightside had recently reached a deal to be acquired as part of a "strategic partnership" with a much bigger, East Coast firm.

So far the transition team from Philadelphia had visited Brightside's SoCal headquarters twice, each time making noncommittal remarks while subtly judging the more laid-back style of dress and conversation on the West Coast. They'd promised to "respect the culture," which, as Preena put it, meant that they planned to change everything about it.

"Try to step it up if you can," Jan said as she signaled that he could go. "The next few weeks are going to mean a lot in terms of evaluations."

Jake thanked his boss and walked outside, promising to improve. He almost expected to find that Sloan had slashed his tires.

His tires were fine, if a little worn on the twelve-year-old Mazda he'd been driving for six years. The best thing he could say about the day so far was that he didn't get a speeding ticket while speeding to the restaurant. Still, by the time he arrived, he hadn't come up with a way to pay down those loans or find a new place to live.

Maybe Maya would have an idea. He'd ask her—after he apologized for being more than thirty minutes late to their anniversary dinner.

2.

He may have been late, and he may have been frazzled. But when he sat down across from Maya, he forgot all about getting evicted from his apartment and nearly losing his job in the same day.

At least for the first thirty seconds.

"Welcome to the Thankful Bistro! How is your energy level tonight?" An incredibly enthusiastic server had appeared in front of him.

"Uh, fine . . . I think?"

"Excellent! What do you have to be thankful for today?"

Jake wondered what had happened to all those normal restaurant questions. *Is tap water okay?* Sure. *Would he like to hear the specials?* That would be great.

He looked at the server, who was wearing a name tag and a sticker on her shirt. The name tag read "Chyna." The sticker had an image of a bee and read "Bee thankful."

"Well, Chyna, today I found out that I owe $50,000 and I'm getting kicked out of my apartment. Oh, and I might lose my job. But otherwise, I'm good."

That's what he thought about saying. But instead he said, "Oh, uh, it's fairly warm for November? Although I guess since we're in California that's not too unusual."

Can we get this over with?

"Is that all you have to be thankful for?" Chyna gave him a wink and looked over at Maya.

Right. Of course.

"It's okay." Maya smiled. "I talked to her while I was waiting and told her it was a special dinner."

Jake pretended to smile at Chyna while silently placing a curse on her family for generations to come.

———

The Thankful Bistro was vegan, but everything on the menu cost as much as the fancy Mexican place he'd been eyeing before Maya picked it. Apparently there was surge pricing on lentils.

Jake took a sip of water and realized he needed to change his attitude. Maybe some of the high-priced positive energy would wear off on him.

Besides, here was Maya. In some ways it felt like it was just yesterday that he bumped into her at the charity event Brightside had helped with. When they sat together during the auction, they whispered nonstop like old friends. After she agreed to go hiking with him the following weekend, he worked extra hard at his job for the next five days, fueled with the anticipation of seeing her again.

In other ways it felt like it had been several years, not six months. He liked her—he *really* liked her. He also didn't want to scare her off. Probably good to not go too fast in these situations, he assumed.

"So, how was your day?" he finally asked.

"It was good!" she said. "I finished up a big report on how our job-training clients are contributing to the local economy. And next weekend we're going to Denver for the regional conference, so I'm helping the new intern get ready."

Maya worked in donor relations for a nonprofit that raised money and support for newly settled immigrants. After college, she'd joined AmeriCorps and worked with kids from migrant families living in East Texas. When she moved back to California she'd jumped into a job with the United Way, changing to a smaller organization after two years because she felt like she could make more of a difference.

What would a future with her look like? At this point, what would *any* future look like? If he didn't get his act together, he wouldn't have many options at all.

"Jake, are you listening?" She had been looking at him for a while.

He came back to life. "Maya, I'm sorry," he said. "To be honest, I had kind of a rough day."

"Well, you do seem really distracted tonight. What happened?"

He told her about the presentation, the messages, and the talk he'd had with Jan on the way out the door. "I'm sure it will be fine," he said when he was finished. He wasn't sure at all, but he worried about dumping his problems on Maya. Among other things, he hadn't told her about the debt before. In his telling now, it became "some student loans from when I was at Cal State," not $50,000 worth.

It still didn't sound great, he realized. But hopefully she understood that he was under some stress. If he could just get a handle on his problems, he'd be able to do a much better job in the boyfriend department.

Time to change the subject. "Hey, are you still planning to invite me for Thanksgiving?"

They were at a crucial stage of their relationship. She'd met Zach, and talked with his parents on a video call before Jake went up for his last visit. But he still hadn't met her family. When she suggested he join her for the upcoming holiday, it felt like a big deal.

She looked away for a moment. "Sure, that would be fine."

That would be fine. Was it his imagination, or did she sound less than enthusiastic?

"Okay, cool. I'm really excited about the tamales!"

He probably should have said something about being excited to meet her family. Still, he *was* really excited about the tamales. She'd told him about a recipe that her grandmother had passed on to her mother. At every holiday, they served a range of traditional Mexican fare along with American standards.

Jake did his best to perk up for the rest of the dinner. For dessert, they ordered a $20 gluten-free vegan apple pie. It was good, as long as you enjoyed the taste of cardboard. But when he looked at Maya and saw that she was perfectly content, he relaxed again. He really should stop complaining so much.

———

When the bill came, he put down his card without looking at the total and went to the bathroom. Returning to the table, he found Chyna sitting in his seat, leaning into conversation with Maya.

"Your girlfriend is amazing!" she said. "She was just giving me advice on skin care. I've been looking for a more organic face wash forever!"

"Sure," he said with another forced smile. "And please get out of my chair."

He didn't actually say that last part. But he felt confident he had communicated it telepathically.

"By the way, Jake," said Maya, "there was some problem with your card not going through. It's not a big deal and I took care of the bill, but you might want to check with the bank tomorrow."

What? Now his debit card wasn't working?

He was sure he had at least $200 in his checking account. Unless . . . the autodebit for his gym membership had gone through on the same day his utility bill did. He'd probably need to cancel that. The gym membership, not the utilities—though come to think of it, technically speaking he wouldn't need electricity at his apartment for much longer either. Still, he didn't realize he was that short on cash.

"Thanks," he said. "Listen, I feel really bad about this." Chyna had moved away from the table and was pretending not to listen while she absorbed every word.

"This was supposed to be a special night, and I've been so distracted. First I was late, and then you ended up paying for dinner."

"It's okay, Jake. I know you had a hard day." Something sounded distant in her voice.

"Can I make it up to you?" he asked hopefully. "I'll pay you back for this, but I'd also like the chance for a do-over."

"Of course. Let's talk more later."

Jake walked her to her car and said good night. Then he got in the Mazda and drove to the apartment that he wouldn't call home for much longer.

Live to fight another day, he thought. Except this was a day he didn't want to repeat anytime soon.

3.

This is your life, Jake. You need to get it together.

It wasn't an audible voice from the heavens that spurred Jake on. It came from his daydreaming self, the one that got him into trouble when he was in client meetings. Out on the jogging track, though, he was safe. There were no clients, no boss, and no one to bother him.

Most of the time, there were no distractions at all. He ran out here three times a week, early in the morning or late in the afternoon when he finished at work. Some people got bored running on a track, but Jake liked the rhythm of it. He had it down to a formula: twenty-four laps, six miles, and forty-five minutes. The track was less than five minutes from his apartment—at least for now—so if he factored in a quick shower, the whole process took just over an hour.

He finished his first mile and settled into a groove.

Alright, where were we . . . oh, that's right. We were broke and losing our apartment. We weren't exactly crushing it at work either.

In times of trial, some people panic. Others flail about, trying different solutions without addressing the real problem. Still others simply give up.

Truth be told, Jake did all of those things from time to time. But he also had another approach. When he found himself in trouble, he would make a list.

Today's list started in his head, legal pads and pens being hard to come by on the jogging track. He began by writing down the trifecta of problems he'd encountered the day before.

1. Have to move out in eighteen days—oh wait, now it's seventeen.
2. Need to start paying off all those loans. I wonder where all the money went?
3. Not doing so great at Brightside, the job I was so excited to get at the beginning of the year.

For now, he decided to defer the last problem. He had an idea to try a different tactic when he was back on Monday, so he'd look at that more then.

Focusing on the first two problems, he made another list in his mind as he rounded the track. He called this list "Assets." It was a pretty short list.

When he'd checked his phone after the previous night's dinner, he had a notification from the bank: "You have attempted to overdraw your account. For your security, we have rejected the charge."

For his security and his embarrassment, he thought.

Not only had he misjudged the timing of those automatic deductions from the gym and the utility company, he'd completely forgotten about another one from his dentist. He was still paying off a $2,000 double root canal from three months earlier. They'd let him split up the payments, but that just meant he'd relive the pain of that morning in the chair every month for the next six.

It wasn't all bad news, though. Hitting his stride on mile three, Jake realized that even if his list of assets was light on financials, he was still doing pretty well elsewhere. He had good health, for one—aside from that root canal. He had parents who'd raised him well, even if they didn't always understand his way of doing things.

Zach was not only his older brother, he was also a close friend. Later today he'd see him, when Jake drove up to the Bay Area so they could have a late lunch. Zach worked for Titan, one of the most successful startups of the past decade. Maybe Jake could get his advice . . . and now that he thought about it, his brother had mentioned he had some news to share.

Liza, their sister, was in her last year of high school. Jake prided himself on being a good big brother, screening potential boyfriends on social media and checking on her every few days.

And then there was Maya. He still wasn't sure what she saw in him, but he wasn't going to question it. He just hoped she wouldn't run away when she eventually figured out how much lower he rated compared to her.

He felt bad about the previous night. That morning he'd texted her another apology along with a photo of a dog holding a bouquet of flowers. When she wrote back with a smiley face and a heart emoji, he instantly felt better.

That was Maya: solid, reliable, and forgiving. It was too soon in their relationship to think long-term—when mentioning his apartment situation, Jake had carefully avoided any suggestion about moving in with her—but he liked her more than he'd ever liked anyone before.

The greatest assets in his life were his relationships, he observed. Unfortunately, those assets couldn't do much to solve his cash flow problems. He was firmly resolved not to ask his family for financial help.

———

As he finished mile four, he considered possible solutions. First, he could cut back on his spending. Did he really need the gym membership? It was good for cross-training, but most of his workouts were right here on the track. There were probably some other subscriptions he could cancel, some $5 lattes he could downsize to the free coffee in the office.

Still, he realized that economizing would only get him so far. He could save some cash here and there, but he was already fairly frugal. And with holidays coming up, he couldn't cut out gifts for Zach, Liza, their parents, and Maya.

The far greater problem was that there wasn't much money in the account to start with. *When you cut back to basics and are still short every month*, he thought, *cutting further isn't going to help very much.*

On the job front, Brightside wasn't going to be offering a raise anytime soon. In fact, the less attention they paid to his performance at this point, the better. He needed to keep the job for the steady paycheck and insurance, but it wasn't enough.

So what could he do—get a second job?

He wasn't opposed to the idea. He liked to work hard, and back in college he'd often held two jobs while juggling classes. But as he added up the figures in his head, he felt discouraged. Most part-time jobs aren't known for paying good wages. Even if he worked an extra fifteen hours a week, he'd still just be getting by.

What he needed to do was *get ahead*. He didn't want to be obsessed with small things. Ultimately, he wanted a lot more for his life. As a kid, he'd had all sorts of dreams and ideas. Lately, though, he felt like he was just struggling to stay afloat.

In the fifth mile, he sharpened his focus and ran faster. He didn't have a long list of problems, he realized. He just had one big problem. It wasn't complicated, it was simple: *his monthly paycheck didn't have a large enough number on it.*

If he had more money, he could find another place to live. Sure, it might be a hassle, but in the end moving was just about packing up your stuff and carting it over to another place. If he had more money, he wouldn't stress about the loan payments. The worst thing about a root canal would be the three hours in the dental chair, not the six months of paying for it afterward. And if he wasn't always scraping by, he could do things like buy plane tickets for Maya and him to visit her parents at Thanksgiving instead of driving five hours each way.

Maybe he could even begin to save for the future.

Finally, even though having more money technically wouldn't help him keep his job at Brightside, he'd be less worried about losing it. The worst-case scenario wouldn't mean he was out on the street—it would just mean he'd need to find another gig.

That's what it all came down to, he realized. Financial independence. A new way to get paid, preferably in larger-than-small amounts and on a regular basis. Money wasn't the answer to everything, but if he had more money coming in, a lot of things would be a lot easier.

So where's the money tree, Jake?

4.

Getting into Titan was like gaining access to a top-secret CIA vault. Visitors passed through multiple security checks on the way inside. Before you reached the inner lobby, you had to run the gauntlet between two receptionists, each wearing an earset and bearing a tablet.

"Welcome to Titan!" said the one on the left, a bit robotically. *Wel-come to Ti-tan.*

The one on the right coolly appraised him as she handed over her tablet. "Please review our visitor guidelines and sign your name at the bottom."

He scrolled through four screens, each containing a dozen paragraphs written in tiny text. From what he could tell, visitors promised to not divulge any secrets, to refrain from taking or posting photos, and to offer their firstborn child as tribute to Titan's CEO. Jake always found the restrictions on social media use especially ironic. Wasn't this a company that had made billions of dollars getting people to constantly check their online feeds?

Still, once you'd signed your life away and were granted access to the main campus, the top-secret CIA vault turned into the Hotel California of tech companies. The powers that ruled the Titan kingdom did everything they could to keep employees on-site, offering personal trainers, dry cleaning, and a full schedule of social activities that took place in the evenings. Jake always found it to be a jarring transition.

He brightened up when Zach met him at the entrance. Even though they lived just a few hours apart, two months had passed since their last visit. "It's been too long!" they each said at the same time.

After greeting each other with a hug, Zach paused for effect. "So, you ready for the main event?"

"Hell yeah!" said Jake. "I ran six miles this morning, so I'm well prepared."

The main event was lunch, and no visit to Titan was complete without an extended tour of the cafeteria. The company maintained an in-house kitchen that rivaled the better restaurants in the area. If you were following the latest fad diet, you'd find plenty of options to choose from. If you wanted something more nostalgic, they had that covered, too—no matter if nostalgia for you came in the form of blueberry pancakes or *masala dosas*.

Jake had learned to not eat breakfast before coming for lunch. Best of all: it was all free. You just walked in and took whatever you wanted. The first time he'd visited, he was amazed. He kept expecting the robotic receptionists to lock the doors and refuse to let him leave until he'd washed dishes for a year.

This was his fourth visit, and by now he understood the quid pro quo. If you were going to sign away your life to enter the building, you might as well enjoy a nice meal while you were there.

They loaded their plates with farm-fresh vegetables and a spicy Thai curry. When they set them down and went back for beverages, Zach steered them to a kombucha station that had been recently installed. It offered a choice between two flavors, hazelnut–goji berry and mango-lime. A smiling server asked which one they'd like to try.

When Jake hesitated, she explained that one was better for mental clarity, and the other could help him feel less anxious.

"Do you have one that will make my student loan payment?" he asked.

When she didn't answer, he pointed to the one on the right. Feeling less anxious couldn't hurt.

———

Jake settled in to enjoy the best lunch he'd had since the last time he was here. *If only I lived closer,* he thought, *I could cut waaay back on meal expenses.*

"So, Zach, what was it you wanted to tell me?" On the phone he'd mentioned he had some big news.

"Let's not talk about it here," Zach said. "I never know who's listening."

"Wow, okay." It really was like the CIA, just with better food and free dry cleaning. For the rest of the meal they talked about other things. Liza, their sister, was graduating high school next year. Instead of going to college right away, she was planning to take a gap year, traveling through Asia and volunteering in different countries. Jake and Zach were hoping to give her a surprise present at Christmas: an offer to pay for her first month's worth of hostel stays. It was another thing Jake worried about—Liza deserved it, and he wanted to be a good brother—but where would the money come from?

They finished their lunch and went outside, stopping by a picnic table that offered a plate of enormous chocolate chip cookies sprinkled with sea salt. It was instinctual: they each reached over to grab one, flashing each other a smile as they did. Meanwhile, a guy from engineering who looked like he hadn't seen the sun in a while was stashing extras in his backpack.

"This is how they keep you!" the pale engineer said as he staggered off.

On a Saturday, the place was less crowded, but not by much. The parking lot was filled with BMWs and Teslas that spent most of their time off duty. Near the main entrance, a fleet of roving shuttles carried employees to and from downtown. Company policy "encouraged" them to use the shuttles, not least of all because the vehicles were equipped with high-speed internet and would allow people to work during their commute.

When the coast was clear, Zach looked up. "Here's the thing, Jake. This is my last month at Titan." He spoke in a low voice as they walked on the lawn. "I'm going to join a new company that's in the process of getting funded."

"Whoa! That *is* big news!" Jake said. "This place always felt like a combination of prison and day care to me. I never thought you'd leave."

"Ha, yeah. It has its perks. But I really want to be part of pioneering something, and I think I've found the next big thing. Do you remember Kevin?"

Of course he did. How could he forget Kevin Quan? Zach and his freshman college roommate had kept in touch even when they moved out of the dorms and to separate apartments. After graduation, Zach went to Titan and Kevin went back to Singapore, where his family was from.

Kevin was not someone you could erase from memory. Always enthusiastic to the point of being hard to handle, Jake's impression was that he was best enjoyed in small doses.

One time Zach went to Las Vegas with a group of Kevin's friends, and they ended up getting into trouble. Jake never heard how it started, but he knew it ended with all of them withdrawing money from an ATM to bail Kevin out of jail. All that was missing from the story was Mike Tyson and a live tiger.

"I know he can be hard to handle sometimes," Zach said, "but he's got a big vision for a new social network called Buzzard. Not only that, but he's managed to land a first round of funding of $20 million from some big-shot venture capitalist. There's a team of twelve right now, and if I enter at this stage, I'll get paid in equity and can come out the other side with enough money to do whatever I want."

"Congrats, man. That's really great." Jake was genuinely happy for him.

"Thanks! I'm giving my notice next week. But hey—what about you? You doing okay down there?"

Jake told him a little about the problems. Just like he did with Maya, he left out some pesky details. He hadn't told anyone in his family the full extent of the loans he'd taken. Zach had been on scholarship at Stanford, and their parents assumed that Cal State's lower tuition meant that Jake was able to pay his way through without borrowing.

Still, he trusted Zach. He told him about his upcoming eviction, and about the fact that he didn't exactly have a lot of cash on hand.

"Anything I can help with?" Zach looked concerned.

For a moment, Jake thought about asking for a loan. But he held back. Visiting the high-powered campus where his brother worked always brought up mixed emotions. Part of him felt rejected by the fact that Zach had been recruited by Titan and not him. Another part of him knew that he didn't belong here.

"Well, you probably can't get me an unlimited pass to the Titan cafeteria once you don't work here anymore. But seriously, it's just good to know you're around if I need to talk things through."

"Of course," Zach said. "By the way, how's Maya?"

"She's good!" Jake said automatically. "We just went to dinner last night, and I'm planning to meet her family at Thanksgiving."

Now that he thought of it, he realized he hadn't heard from Maya since her message early that morning. They usually made plans for Sunday after she'd had brunch with friends from her college sorority. He reminded himself to call her when he was driving back after lunch.

On the way out, Jake found his old Mazda parked where he left it between a long line of low-mileage German cars. He glanced at the backseat as he unlocked the door.

I wonder if there's enough room to sleep there.

Better not cancel that gym membership after all. If he started living out of his car, he'd need a place to shower.

He called out to Zach as his brother walked back toward the campus. "Hey, one more thing! On your last day here, can you bring me some of those cookies?"

5.

When Monday morning rolled around, Jake was ready to shake it off. He still wasn't sure what to do about the apartment—the countdown to eviction now stood at T-minus fifteen days—but he decided to defer that worry in favor of making up for his poor performance at work on Friday.

Running his miles on the track that morning, he'd thought more about Avery Tech's problems. Sales were down . . . and not by a little. Looking at the company's analytics to see what customers were searching for wasn't a bad idea, but it wouldn't solve everything. He used his daydreaming time to consider a number of different ideas for how they could turn things around. This was, after all, what he was supposed to be good at.

After he'd showered and got settled at work, he planned to type up his notes and wrangle a second chance to make a better impression. The first item on his schedule was a conference call with Magnate, the larger agency in Philadelphia that was "sort of merging" with Brightside. Since the call wasn't until eleven, he didn't think much about it while he was running his laps.

As soon as he arrived at the office, though, he knew something wasn't right. Preena, Sloan, and several other colleagues were nowhere to be seen. Was he really the first one here? He couldn't be *late* . . . he'd double-checked the call invitation that morning and confirmed it started at eleven a.m. It wasn't even eight thirty yet.

He poked his head into Jan's office and saw them all sitting there, focused on a speakerphone positioned in the middle of the table. Sloan looked up and flashed a fake smile. "He's awake! Good of you to join us, Jake."

"What are you guys doing? I thought we weren't starting until—"

"Eleven a.m. Eastern time, Jake," Preena mouthed at him while looking up. "It's three hours later over there."

Eastern time, of course. How could he have missed that?

"Wow, I'm really sorry, everyone. I must have misread the invite . . ." He tried to rally. "But I did have some ideas to share, whenever the group is ready."

"Jake, we're just in the middle of something." Jan spoke up. "Take a seat, or—" She looked around, but all the chairs were taken. "Or just stand over there until we finish."

For the rest of the call, he stood in the corner. The metaphor was obvious. All he needed was a time-out chair and for Jan to take away his phone for the rest of the week.

The CEO of Magnate was talking about a new assessment tool the whole company would be using during the transition. Jake didn't catch all the references, but he noticed everyone else was paying close attention and taking notes. When the call ended, Jan asked her assistant to step out so that Jake could take her chair.

"Hey," he started to say, "I just want to apologize to everyone again. I really thought the call was later."

Jan waved it off. "To be honest, this one wasn't that important. Client work matters more. But here's what *is* important," she continued. "There's good news and bad news coming out of the merger-nonmerger. Good news is, they're keeping the West Coast office, at least in some form." She paused. "The bad news is, there won't be room for everyone. As part of the consolidation effort, you'll all be assessed on your performance."

"That's what everyone was taking notes on when you came in," Preena said. "The system is totally automated. Basically, it ranks everyone according to their performance, and then automatically recommends the lowest-ranked people for dismissal."

"It sounds like *The Office* meets *Game of Thrones*," Jake said, and a few people chuckled.

"I know, isn't it great? You never know who's going to get an ax to the skull." That was from Sloan, who seemed truly excited about the idea.

"Alright, let's get to work," said Jan, drawing the meeting to a close. "We need to put on a good show this week."

———

Jake tailed Preena out of Jan's office again as they walked back to their desks. He was determined to regroup on yet another failure in front of the team, and this time he had an idea—but it turned out that she had one, too.

"Hey, Jake." She stopped him before they split off to work on separate tasks. "There's something I wanted to talk with you about on Friday. With your housing crisis and those loans coming due, I figured you're in need of extra money."

He nodded. "Yeah, I was hoping for a money tree to sprout from the ground and solve all my problems, but . . ."

"Ha. Well, you're not the only one with money on your mind!" she said.

Preena told him that she was learning to make and sell hand-crafted jewelry and had already earned a few thousand dollars since starting. Before last week, Jake would have thought this was mildly interesting. Now, it suddenly sounded a lot more relevant. He didn't know much about jewelry, but a few thousand dollars was real money. Maybe there was something he could learn.

"That's awesome," he said. "How did you learn to do it?"

"I started going to a group that meets every week to talk through different strategies and projects. It's called the Third Way."

"It sounds like a cult," Jake said, ever the skeptic.

Preena rolled her eyes. "It's legit. And here's the thing. Ever since I went to Bali for my yoga retreat last year, I've been wanting to go back. Next time, I'd love to be able to take more of an extended leave and spend a whole month there. I guess we'll need to see how this assessment thing turns out, but if I still have a job I'd like to ask for an unpaid sabbatical. The only problem with an unpaid sabbatical," she continued, "is that whole 'unpaid' part. So I figured I needed to make some money that I wasn't already budgeting elsewhere. And the more I thought about it, the more I realized I should probably be doing that anyway. These days, it's not smart to rely on a single company for your entire income."

"That's exactly what I've been thinking about," said Jake. "I thought about signing up for one of those ride-sharing programs, but when I did the math I realized I wouldn't make much more than minimum wage. They promise that you'll be an 'owner,' but they're the ones collecting most of the money while all the drivers are out hustling."

"Right," said Preena. "So that's what brought me to the Third Way, the group I've been going to. It's a bunch of people who are all trying to make money on the side, but not in a way where they're just getting part-time jobs working for someone else."

"Okay, fair enough. It's not a cult. So it's like . . . an incubator for startups?"

"Not exactly. More like a place where regular people can learn together. Everyone there is trying to get something going for themselves, without quitting their day jobs."

"Huh," he said. "I've never really thought of myself as an entrepreneur, but I like that approach. How much does it cost?"

Preena laughed. "I was skeptical, too! But not only is it free, they also have a guiding value: *the less you spend on your project, the better*. It's a way of adding a challenge while also making sure that you don't waste money while you're learning. Most people end up spending less than $500."

"And you can start a business with that?"

"Sometimes even less. Why don't you come and check it out? I think you'd like the founder."

"Sure, okay," Jake said. "I definitely need to do *something*. And if this group happens to have a spare apartment in the back of the meeting space, I wouldn't object."

———

Jake wasn't sure he'd find the answers he needed in a group, but he promised himself he'd approach it with an open mind. It couldn't hurt. But first things first: in an effort to redeem himself for his morning tardiness—not to mention Friday's screwup—he worked through lunch typing up the notes with his ideas for Avery Tech.

He took the printout to Jan, who was talking on the phone but waved him in. When she finished, he handed her a six-page report.

"This is a freebie," he told her. "It's up to you whether you want to bill Avery for it or not, but I worked on it over the weekend and just now during the lunch break, so it won't cost the company any of my time."

The report was titled "How Avery Tech Can Sell More and Keep Customers Longer." Jan leafed through it and was impressed. It featured a list of eight detailed suggestions Jake had compiled, based on comparisons with its competitors and the results of a customer survey the company had conducted. Properly implemented, it looked like any one of the suggestions could give Avery a real boost.

"Jake, this is great," she said, underlining a couple of sentences as she turned the pages. "You just whipped this up?"

"Well, it's part of what I was thinking about last week but didn't explain very well. After the meeting, I put more time into it to make sure it had a chance to see the light of day."

She nodded. "I'll do what I can to make sure they look at it. But remember that the new assessment tool won't measure anything creative like this. What matters is billable hours and new accounts. There's also a 360 review system where we ask some of your peers to provide constructive feedback."

Perfect. Can't wait for Sloan's "constructive" feedback.

"Jake, don't get me wrong," she went on. "I like you, and I hope you'll be able to stick around. But you need to understand that this is a model where managers have only limited input. There's a real chance some people will be out of a job, and soon. I want you to be prepared for that reality."

He left Jan's office feeling like a tennis player who had come from behind and battled to a fifth set, only to lose the championship in a tie breaker. He'd done everything he could in preparing that report, and now it looked like it wouldn't matter.

Back at his desk, he had another message from Roland, the property manager. There had been a surge of interest in his apartment, and they'd scheduled viewings for four of the next five days. "We don't want this to be an inconvenience to you," Roland said. "But if you could manage to stay out of the unit until 9:00 p.m. each day, the family would appreciate it. Also, please make sure everything is nice and tidy before you leave in the mornings. There will be a lot of people coming in and out."

Jake made a mental note to put his entire life on hold until he found a new place to live. Then, by habit, he checked his bank account to see if his paycheck had been deposited yet. No luck. He was still sitting on less than $2,500 to his name, or negative $50,000 if you factored in those loans that were coming due.

It was clear that something had to change, and soon.

6.

"This meeting is called to order. Our first item of business is . . . Indonesian Sumatra Gold!"

Clarence, the group's leader, passed out small cups of strong dark coffee. Most of the eight people in the room took one, with the first cup being passed to Jake.

"Welcome!" Clarence said to him. "Preena said you needed to be here."

He almost hadn't come tonight. Walking into a roomful of strangers was never at the top of his list of ideal ways to spend an evening. As an introvert, the daily interaction at work forced his capacity to the max. It wasn't just the client calls and presentations,

it was all the unwritten expectations of "team building" and social-
izing that drained him.

Privately, he'd also wondered if it would be weird. Would someone ask him about his chakras, or expect him to say he was thankful
about being in debt and close to homelessness? Worse, what if they
asked him to share his business ideas? He didn't have any!

But in the end, he'd kept his promise to Preena and went along
with her after work. At least his debit card wouldn't be declined,
since the meeting was free. And it's good that he did, because what
happened next marked the beginning of a transformation. Years
later, he'd look back and reflect on how this one casual decision
had changed his life forever.

It started with the coffee. Clarence was into it. *Really* into it. In
his early fifties, he was fit and active, with the energy of a younger
man and a keen sense of self-discipline that had carried over from
a stint in the military decades earlier. His dark brown eyes lit up as
he told the group about the origin of this week's brew.

Jake liked coffee as much as anyone else. He bought a latte most
mornings and would grab a cup or two later in the day from the
office machine. But he wasn't sure he'd ever tasted coffee this good
before. It was delicious. It was also *strong*.

The others in the group were equally enthusiastic. "I don't get
much sleep on Thursday nights," said Adrian, a lanky Asian guy
sitting next to him. "But I'm not sure it's just the coffee. I always
leave with ideas bouncing around in my head."

"Is there a decaf option?" Jake asked.

"Clarence doesn't believe in decaf." That was from Preena, who'd introduced Jake to the group. When they finished work earlier, they slurped down a quick bowl of noodles and drove to a coworking space that served as the meeting point.

"Alright, everyone!" Clarence took control of the room. Although he was soft-spoken, there was something about the way he carried himself that caused everyone around him to pay attention when he was talking. It was a gentle, yet effective, style of leadership.

"I'm glad you like the coffee," he said. "This is one of my favorite new blends. But let's get down to business. Before we jump in, Jake, welcome to the Third Way. We're always happy to have new folks with us."

"At least if you're willing to work," said Jo, a woman who spoke with an accent he couldn't quite place.

"Well, that's true," agreed Clarence. "We don't want any spectators. Everyone is here because they want to make extra money in a smart way. The best way to learn how to do that is to jump right in."

"Adrian, can you explain the purpose of the group? Jake, I'll send you a digital copy of our manifesto after the meeting, but let's make sure you have the quick version first."

"Sure," Adrian said. "It's pretty simple. Like Clarence said, everyone here wants to make more money. And we want to do it without just getting another job. In other words, we're all trying to start a business of some kind.

"Each of us has a different reason for *why* this is important. Me, for example . . . I've been working in finance for fifteen years, and I'm ready for a change. I'd really like to go full-time with a mobile app I've been building. But I also have a family to support, so I can't just quit my job without a safety net. I'm hoping to build up the income over the next year, and *then* take the leap."

Marta, a middle-aged Filipino woman, jumped in. "My goal is different. I really like my job. I do neuroscience research at the university, and I enjoy mentoring grad students."

Jake nodded as she went on.

"I'm not trying to go all in, but at the same time, I love being able to get paid more than once. Last month I earned an extra $1,500 by doing test-prep coaching. I can't live off $1,500 a month in California, and I make a lot more than that at my job . . . but still, there's something about that money that just feels different."

"It's because you made it on your own," said Jo, and everyone agreed.

"Anyway," Adrian said, "the reasons why we're each here tend to vary, but the goal is the same. We all want to create a moneymaking asset for ourselves—kind of like some people do with buying rental properties, but without spending much money or going into debt."

"And one more thing," interjected Celia, who had started to tell Jake about her travel website before the meeting started. "Everything we do is based around a simple principle. Right, everyone?"

They all nodded. "That principle is . . ."

"YOU CAN DO MORE THAN YOU THINK," several people spoke at once.

Clarence smiled. "Indeed, that's the most important principle of all! Okay, thanks for the summary. It's also important that everyone is as open and honest as possible. We talk about real stuff here, including being transparent about any mistakes we make. Now shall we jump into story time?"

Jake raised his hand. "Just one question. This all sounds really great . . . but why is it called the Third Way?"

"You're right, I guess we didn't discuss that." Clarence paused. "Jake, let's plan to talk a bit more later so you have the whole story. The short version is that we're using a model that's different from the old, traditional way of starting a business. It's also distinct from what companies do in the so-called startup world, so that's why we call it the Third Way."

He sat back down and looked around the room. "But just like with everything else, you'll probably learn more by doing than talking. So who's first?"

———

Celia spoke up. "I'll go first. I've got an update about Hotel Highlight." The group turned to look at her.

"I've made a lot more progress since last week. I want to create a travel blog for women that focuses on boutique hotel reviews. I know this market well, and I don't think any current mainstream publication really meets their needs."

"Sounds good," said Clarence. "And remind us . . . how will it make money?"

"Through affiliate commissions. When users click through to make a booking at a hotel I recommend, I'll earn a small fee. It's not a lot per booking, but if I get enough users making enough bookings, it can add up."

Adrian spoke up. "The commission model is great, but what if you also offered sponsored blog posts, where hotels pay to be featured? If you had a lot of traffic, that could be valuable to them."

"Yeah," said Preena, jumping in. "But it would be important to maintain your independence, so that you keep the trust of your visitors. In the end, that's the most valuable asset you have."

"I agree," Celia replied. "I'm looking at some kind of combination of those two. However, here's the problem: for either option to work well, I'll need a significant user base. The last project I tried struggled with that limitation, so I want to have a plan for it before jumping in."

"Very smart," Clarence said. "Let's spend some time thinking about how you might build a strong audience early on . . . maybe something like three thousand registered users in the first sixty days."

The group went back and forth, tossing around ideas, adding to one another's comments, and occasionally disagreeing. Clarence guided the discussion, but didn't usually say much until it was time to move to the next person.

Next up was Jo, who said that she had grown up in eastern Europe and now worked as a pharmaceutical sales rep. On the side, she made and sold dollhouse furniture. "I got into it for some of the same reasons other people have talked about," she said. "But for me it was also important to do something creative. All day long I talk on the phone and visit doctors' offices. I wanted to actually *make* something, and I loved dollhouses when I was a kid."

Jo's problem was different from Celia's. She already had a committed base of buyers and was making a profit of $3,000 per month. She felt like she could be doing more for them, but she had too many ideas and not enough time to implement them.

"I'm struggling to understand what's most important," she said at the end.

Finally, Adrian gave an update about his app. He was also doing well, having made $5,000 so far after expenses, but trying to navigate a tough decision. He planned to introduce a free version of the app to attract more downloads, but wanted to make sure it didn't take away from the sales of the paid version.

They spent the better part of two hours discussing the issues that Celia, Jo, and Adrian raised. The whole time, Jake was writing a flurry of notes. Since he worked in marketing for his job, he understood most of what they were talking about. He noticed, however, that they tended to use different language than he did with corporate clients. For example, they didn't talk a lot about big, strategic mission plans. The discussion was much more practical, typically based around simple questions like "Would someone buy this?" And they almost never referred to investors or said anything about "raising capital."

I guess it's because everyone here is doing it on their own, and without spending much money . . . which is how I'd need to do it, too.

Before the group wrapped up, Clarence turned to him. "Jake, do you mind telling us a little about why you're here?"

"No problem," he said. "And thanks for being so welcoming, everyone. Preena told me how much she was learning from this group. I don't really have any ideas yet, but I'm hoping to figure something out.

"Long story short, the other day I learned that I need to start repaying $50,000 in student loans I've been ignoring since graduation. I'm also losing my apartment . . . and I might lose my job. Then there's climate change, the earthquake that's eventually going to take out California, and the latest war in the Middle East. But aside from that, everything else is going great!"

The group laughed.

"Seriously, though," he concluded, "I need to make some money."

Everyone at the long table nodded in understanding. "We get it," Adrian said. "Money's not everything in life, but when you don't have it, you have less control. You have fewer choices."

"Exactly!" Jake said. "I'm not trying to start a hedge fund, but it would be great to pay back my loans and rent a new place without stressing out so much. And I should probably call my girlfriend more often, but I suppose that's out of scope for this meeting."

More laughter. "That's right, Jake," said Clarence. "You're on your own for that one. But if your girlfriend likes dollhouses, maybe you should buy some furniture from Jo, or book her a hotel from Celia's website."

Clarence looked at his phone. "Okay, everyone, it's getting late. Feel free to post your notes and any questions in the online forum. And Jake, let's see if we can bring you up to speed a bit more."

———

The group broke up, with everyone looking wide awake after an intense discussion and a second serving of the Indonesian Sumatra.

Jake followed up on Clarence's invitation. "Thanks again for welcoming me here," he said as they packed up. "I can tell this could be good for me, but I don't really know what to do next."

"I understand," said Clarence. "The best way to do it is to jump right in, but it does help to have some initial direction. I have an assignment that will be perfect for you. Can you meet early tomorrow morning?"

He hadn't been expecting Clarence to offer a private meeting, and Jake didn't have a lot of spare time for assignments these days. But he also knew he'd been putting off the reality of his situation long enough. "Okay!" he agreed, adding the appointment to his phone.

"Great, I'll send you a link to the place. How about six thirty? That way we can talk for an hour and still have time for a full workday. Just be sure to check the time zone . . ."

Jake covered his head in mock shame. When introducing him to the group earlier, Preena had good-naturedly told the story of his missed meeting.

"Don't worry," he said. "This is far more important than any conference call. I'll be there."

—Interlude—

From: Clarence Johnson

From: Clarence Johnson

To: Jake Aarons

Subject: Manifesto

Jake, I look forward to our meeting tomorrow. Here's that document I mentioned. It provides some background about how we approach projects.

We'll talk more in a few hours, so you don't need to memorize this. But it might be good to take a quick look before we meet. Everything we do is based on these simple principles.

Get some sleep and I'll see you at Lava Java bright and early!

Best,

Clarence

The Third Way
A Manifesto

No one should depend on a single paycheck for their entire income. And now, there's no good reason why you have to.

Whether you call it a side hustle, a small business, or just "something you do for extra money," you can use this model to create more freedom for yourself.

To start, follow these five guiding principles. If you get stuck, come back to them. The answer is probably found in some part of the model.*

1. Everyone's an expert at something.

One way or another, you have acquired a lot of valuable knowledge throughout your life. Something you already know about can be turned into cash—you just need to figure out how to do it.

Don't invest tens of thousands of dollars in business school. Start by taking an inventory of your skills, including everything that you're good at and any topics that people frequently ask you about.

2. Go from idea to product or service.

When you're thinking of ideas to make money, always think of them in specific, concrete terms. One of the people in our group is selling dollhouse furniture. If you go to her website, you can see exactly what she's selling, how much it costs, and how to place an order.

Don't be vague—tell people exactly what you're offering, why it will help them, and how they can buy it.

3. Spend as little money as possible.

Starting frugally is a benefit, not a limitation. The time to "invest in your business" is when you know you have a proven idea. Otherwise, spend more time working on the idea. The vast majority of Third Way projects can be started for less than $500, and sometimes without spending any money at all.

4. Launch before you're ready.

You won't get the feedback you really need until you have something to show. As a general rule, you can have a workable version of most income-generating projects up and running within thirty days. Following this principle also helps you select the most basic iteration of your idea. You can improve it or ramp up later—first, see if it has real potential.

5. Improve as you go.

Based on what you learn, make changes. Don't be afraid to completely restructure—giving up on one project and starting another is A-OK. And when something's working, double down and figure out how to make it work *more*.

In short, keep your risk low, act quickly, and adjust as you go along. Last but not least . . . *you can do more than you think!*

* Get a free set of tools and resources at MoneyTreeBook.com.

7.

Jake was sleepy, but tried to pull it together. When he arrived at the Lava Java the next day at 6:28 a.m., he found Clarence already inside, chatting with the barista and holding an extra cup, which he handed to Jake. They moved over to a shared table, and Clarence jumped in right away.

"Glad you made it. Did you take a peek at the email I sent? . . . Good. So yesterday you asked about the Third Way. It's a good question. To answer it properly, let's begin by looking at how things used to work when someone opened a small business. When you think about a traditional business run by just one person, what do you think of?"

Jake thought for a moment. "Hm . . . like a mom-and-pop shop? Some kind of retail store, or a service like a dry cleaner?"

"Exactly. All of those examples work. Let's take your first one and imagine we're opening a place like this coffee shop. What would we need to do that?"

The Lava Java was located in a strip mall about ten minutes from downtown. It wasn't prime real estate, but the area was close to lots of businesses.

"Well," Jake began, "you'd need all the fancy coffee equipment, which doesn't look like it comes cheap. You'd need all the cups and glasses and plates, and everything else used by the customers."

"Right, and there's more . . ."

"Yeah. You'd also need all this furniture, the big sign out front to draw in customers . . . and wait, before you needed all that, you'd need an actual store. Like, a place to do business . . ."

Did he really say "like, a place to do business"? Jake shook his head and started to revise his words, but Clarence plowed through.

"Okay, so let's say you find the right place. Do you think you can just walk in and set up shop?"

"No, you'd need to sign a lease. And I'd imagine that most commercial leases are based on a fixed period of time, usually a year or two. To get it for less than that, you'd need to pay more."

"Exactly. But that's not all! So far we haven't talked about employees. Even a small coffee shop like this one usually has at least a couple of part-timers. And if you have employees, then you have all sorts of other costs. You need to pay taxes on their wages. You need to have someone do the payroll and take care of permits."

Jake was taking notes on all the different expenses they'd talked about so far. In the margins of his notebook, he added other costs that came to mind. You can't have a coffee shop without providing Wi-Fi these days, for example. You needed insurance in case there was an accident. And then there were cleaning supplies, flyers for advertising, the payment terminals and fees to take credit cards— and that was just what he'd thought of in the first two minutes.

It all added up to . . . a lot.

"This is my point, Jake." Clarence leaned into the table. "Even something 'small' like this shop isn't small to the people running it. They're taking a lot of risk and putting their heart into it. And the rewards aren't always that lucrative. Sure, they sell more of those expensive milk-and-sugar concoctions than actual coffee these days"—for a moment, Clarence looked legitimately offended—"but with all those costs factored in, profit margins are slim."

"Are you saying that no one should open a small business this way?"

"Not at all! We *need* these coffee shops and other small businesses. If anything, the rest of us should do a better job of supporting them. We shouldn't always go to the chain places that come in and drive up the rent because they can afford to lose money for the sake of growth."

Clarence kept going. "So, no, that's not what I'm saying. What I'm saying is that if you're thinking of starting *any* kind of business, you should think carefully about the costs. And you should ask if there might be a better way. These days there are so many options for making money that you might be much better off not going through all this stress."

Jake was writing all of this down as fast as possible. It made sense that owning a retail establishment wouldn't be the best way to make money quickly, or even at all. Still, if that was the old way, what was the new one? Or, actually, that was *one* of the old ways. Clarence had said there were two.

"I think I understand that. Running a high-cost small business isn't always the smartest move, unless it's what you want to do more than anything else. What about the second way?"

"Didn't you say that your brother works for Titan?" Clarence asked.

"Well, he did—he's actually leaving to work for a small startup. They have something like $20 million in venture capital funding. I'm not exactly sure how that works, but I know there's a lot of pressure on them to scale quickly."

"That's another good example. He can probably tell you more about what that world is like, but the point is that it's very different from starting on your own without debt. The first way is a mom-and-pop business, with money saved up or borrowed from the bank. The second way is the startup model with outside investors.

"So that brings us to the Third Way," he continued, "which is the model that everyone in our group operates from. Our goal is to help people make products and services just like those mom-and-pop retailers do, but without borrowing a lot of money or taking a huge risk. Everyone needs to be able to make money for themselves, even if they plan to keep working a regular job. These days, that's 100 percent possible, but it takes some getting used to if you've always worked for someone else."

Everyone needs to be able to make money for themselves. These days, that's 100 percent possible.

"So, Jake, you have a lot of notes there." It was true; Jake had been writing furiously the whole time, and the last part of what he'd heard seemed particularly important. Meanwhile, Clarence had finished his second cup of coffee and was starting to pack up his things.

"But I didn't bring you here just to give you a theory," he said, spinning the cup in his hand. "I have an assignment for you. You need to make money soon, right?"

"Yep. The sooner, the—"

"I get it. So I hope you don't mind a little tough love. The most important thing I could ever tell you is right in the Third Way mission statement: *you can do more than you think*. So to kick off your challenge, I have a question for you. Ready?"

Jake was fully awake now, at least until the caffeine crash took effect. "Absolutely. Born ready!" He sounded more convinced than he really was, but he figured that showing a little enthusiasm was good.

"Let's say you had to make an extra $1,000 in the next few days. What would you do?"

"Uh . . . I really don't know. If I had an extra $1,000, or if I *knew* how I could get $1,000 whenever I needed, I wouldn't be so stuck."

"Jake, a lot of people around the world are stuck. They can't buy rental properties or invest in the stock market, the way that some so-called experts tell them to do. But they still find a way to get by. What do you think they do?"

Clarence was on a roll, so Jake waited for the answer.

"They buy and sell things! They find a way to make something and then sell it, *or* they buy something that's already made and try to sell it for a higher price."

He settled back in his chair. "So guess what—you can do that, too. And here's a hint: start with an online auction or classified ads site. There are a few big ones that you probably know about, and lots of smaller ones."

Jake felt a little disappointed. The Third Way guru was telling him to sell something through an online auction? Surely he could do better.

"Is that all there is to it?" he asked.

"Well, have you ever tried it?"

"No . . . I guess not. Or actually, my sophomore year of college, I made an account on one of those sites to sell a textbook that I no longer needed. Now that I think about it, I made something like $40, which was great for the ten minutes it took me to mail it to the guy who bought it."

"Do you have any more textbooks lying around, Jake?"

"Yeah, I probably have a few somewhere. Okay, so . . . I understand that I could make some money selling my old stuff. Anything helps at this point. But that will only take me so far. What do I sell when I run out of stuff I already have?"

Clarence checked the time again and stood up. "Jake, I know you're in a jam, but from what I can tell about you already, I also know that you're smart. All I'll say now is that there *is* an answer. If you really, really had to, you could find your way out. So that's your challenge—before the next group meeting, come up with an extra $1,000. And anything you earn from selling something you already own doesn't count."

He got up and walked out, leaving Jake sitting with three pages of notes and no idea what to do next. Somehow he'd have to find a way to rise to the challenge. But how?

8.

At first it sounded like a crazy idea: make $1,000 appear out of thin air, and all before next Thursday rolled around. When he'd asked for a money tree, he hadn't realized he really needed one.

Plus, it wasn't like he had an entire week until the group met again. It was more like five days, and in the meantime he had a full-time job that he would be wise to pay attention to. To give the money tree every opportunity to grow and flourish, he really only had the weekend, plus whatever time he could squeeze in before or after work.

But the more he thought about it, the more he saw the genius of the challenge. If, somehow, he could make $1,000, *he could probably find a way to make more.* The deadline was a benefit—it would force him to stop thinking and start taking action.

Still, what would he do?

Clarence said he should think about "buying and selling." And the textbook thing sounded like a clue.

When he got home that evening, he went straight to his closet, where he kept a bunch of boxes from his last move. He remembered lugging all the heavy books up the steps, stubbing his toe and cursing, but telling himself that he should hang on to them "for reference." Yet here he was, six months later, and those books he loved so much had never been unpacked from their boxes.

Now he was glad he'd kept them, just not for the reason he'd expected. He had nearly a dozen in good condition. If he wasn't sure how he could make $1,000 by selling stuff he didn't own, at least he could start with what he did.

He went and logged on to the auction site he'd used once a few years back. It was easy to make a listing—he simply typed in the title of the first book he picked up, and a lot of prewritten info appeared. He took a photo of the book with his phone and uploaded it to the listing. In the description field, he wrote, "Principles of Economics, Volume I, in good condition. Bid now before demand exceeds supply!"

Then he made the listing live with a minimum bid of $1. The book was worth at least $25, but he thought he might attract more potential buyers with a low starting bid.

He spent the next hour listing eight more books. Before he'd finished, some of the first listings already had bids. Then he took a look at other ones for similar titles, including some that seemed to sell more frequently than others. He noticed an interesting auction that was ending soon. The listing was from a college bookstore that was selling a bulk set of ten textbooks, all the same title.

He guessed that most students didn't need ten copies of the same book, and that was why the auction was set to end in an hour at a price just twice that of the average single copy listing. *Hm.*

Thinking quickly, he put in a bid. An hour later, immersed in other things, he glanced up in surprise when he saw a notification flash across his screen. He'd won the auction! For a brief moment, he felt like he'd picked a set of winning lottery numbers and would soon be posing for a photo with an oversized check. He came back to reality a moment later when he realized this was a lottery he'd need to pay for.

Still, it felt good. He immediately listed two of his newly acquired books for sale. He didn't have them on hand yet, of course, but he was now the owner. He figured he'd just turn them around to the final buyer whenever they arrived in the mail.

He took a short break to grab a burrito from Raul's Taqueria next door, then went straight back to work. He finished late in the evening with fifteen total listings. When he woke up the next morning, more than half of them had bids. Most were fairly low, but for one of his accounting books—the set of ten he'd purchased from the college on a whim—the price was already much higher than the average cost of each book he'd bought as a set. He calculated that at minimum, he'd make $20 on that one sale. If he could continue to replicate the results for the rest of them, he'd end up with a profit of at least $200. *Not bad at all.*

It was working! At least partially. He wasn't going to get rich flipping textbooks, but he could tell he was learning something that would prove even more valuable than whatever he made from the first batch of sales.

That was when something clicked in his mind. If he could buy textbooks for one price and sell them for a higher price, two logical questions presented themselves. First: where could he find *more* textbooks to buy at a price lower than what other buyers were paying? If he bought and sold more books, he'd make more money. Second: what *else* could he buy and sell using this same simple model?

It was that second question that got him thinking the most. During his lunch break at Brightside that day, he peeked at a few websites focused on his local area. Each of them included listings of all sorts of things people were buying and selling. It was a lot to wade through, and he realized he could easily get sucked into a vortex.

So instead of scrolling through thousands of listings from people selling everything from used mattresses to Thomas Kinkade paintings, he decided to specialize. A couple of years ago, he'd gotten into photography and taken a few online classes. It wasn't an active hobby he'd kept up, but he knew a fair amount about the gear. Cameras and lenses were expensive, and there was a whole host of accessories you could buy if you had the money.

He tried searching for "cameras," but that still produced too many results to go through. Getting even more specific, he searched for the particular model he'd owned before handing it over to his sister, Liza, as a long-term loan.

There were seven results, and he took a closer look at each of them. Maybe, out of seven listings, one of them wouldn't be written well, or the camera would have a minor flaw that could easily be corrected, or it would otherwise stand out as being underpriced. Then, he could snatch it up and resell it for more.

When lunch ended, he had to pry himself away from the search to get back to client work. He did, after all, still have a job. At least for the moment.

———

He spent most of Friday night with a legal pad full of notes. Two dozen browser tabs fought for real estate space on his laptop while he scanned through items for sale.

In just a few hours, he'd already noticed some trends. His economics and accounting textbooks were seeing a lot of action. His *Survey of Western Civilization* primer, not so much. Good thing he'd doubled down on economics when buying that bulk order. *Sell what people want to buy* was proving to be a valuable lesson.

By now, he'd also made another plan for the weekend—or in fact, Preena had suggested it to him. "It's great that you're looking online," she'd said. "But what about all the places people gather to sell their stuff in person? There might be less competition, and more opportunity for retail arbitrage."

Retail arbitrage. That's interesting.

He didn't think he'd ever heard that phrase before, but he liked the sound of it. Arbitrage was the act of taking advantage of price differences. Big financial companies did it to make money on stocks and commodities. Jake could do it on cameras, textbooks, and maybe whatever else he found along the way.

That night, he set his alarm for another early morning. Operation Yard Sale Arbitrage would begin at dawn. Before he fell asleep, he couldn't resist one last peek at his phone. Two more sales had gone through, and he'd made another $47 in profit.

Not looking at his phone when money was coming in was going to be a hard habit to break—but it was a lot better than being stressed about *no* money. At least now, something was happening.

9.

Saturday morning, Jake hit the ground running. He had a list of local yard sales and flea markets and arrived at his first stop just before the announced opening of eight a.m.

He joined the line behind a small crowd of old-timers who looked like elderly gang members trying to protect their turf. They looked him up and down and just nodded when he said good morning.

Oh well. He had better things to do than worry about being hazed by the yard sale fraternity. He had to find stuff to sell!

By his third stop, he had it down. He'd start by making a quick loop of the yard, garage, or market and determine if it was worth further review. If it seemed like it had potential, he'd home in on a few items, discreetly using his phone to check their resale value. If not, he'd jump back in the Mazda and head to the next stop.

At stop number four, he stumbled on a jackpot. In the midst of a pile of used khakis—no, thanks—he found three camera lenses, a gear bag, and several accessories. Everything was in near-mint condition.

The woman running the store explained that her uncle was a photographer and had recently passed away. Jake offered his condolences. Then he offered a fair price for all of the items, factoring in a reasonable discount for picking up everything at once. They struck a deal and he walked off with his loot. Doing some quick calculations, he figured that he'd easily make at least $100 from this one find alone.

At another stop, he bumped into someone who was also looking down at his phone furtively. The man was standing next to a full-size washer and dryer—another category Jake wasn't interested in—and he seemed to be in a hurry. He'd pulled his pickup truck right into the driveway of the house, then hopped out and walked straight over to the appliances.

"You buy and sell these?" Jake asked him.

Pickup Truck Guy looked suspicious. "Why—you in the business?"

Jake pointed at his Mazda. "That's my car, so I don't think you have to worry about me trying to haul this away. It's all yours."

Pickup Truck Guy relaxed. "Right. In that case, nice to meet-cha," he said. He almost smiled, but caught himself just in time and frowned. "My name's Romeo, but call me George."

"Okay, Rom—George. I'm Jake. How did you get into this?"

"Lost my job a few months ago. My cousin felt bad for me, so when he bought a new dryer, he gave me the old one to sell. I think he figured I could make a few bucks, which I did, but I also realized somethin' else. Every week, people in this town are up-grading their kitchens and appliances—and you can't exactly put your old washer and dryer in the recyclin' bin."

He pointed to the appliances on the lawn. "So that's what I do. Get 'em for free when I can, or pay a cheap price whenever some-one's smart enough to ask for payment."

"That's awesome," Jake said. "But there's one part I don't under-stand. Where do they go? How do you sell them after picking them up? You can't exactly put them in a box and drop them off at the post office."

George had turned friendly, but now he clammed up again. "Can't tell ya that. Trade secret! But here's my card . . . look me up if you run into any washers or dryers out there."

With that, he walked back to the truck and drove off without a wave.

Jake looked down at the card.

Romeo (George) S. Sandberger

Large Appliances

ANY CONDITION

I guess there are all kinds of folks in this business.

Five stops later, Jake's Mazda looked like it had won a shopping spree on *The Price Is Right*, at least if there was a version of the show set in a trailer park. He headed home, made himself a quick lunch, then jumped back on his laptop.

He checked the bids on his current listings. In the time he'd been gone, three more auctions had closed. He invoiced the winning bidders and spent the afternoon adding a dozen new listings. This was fun!

———

At the end of Saturday, he did a quick audit of his status. Factoring in the cost of the items purchased, so far he'd already made $270—not bad, but nowhere close to the $1,000 goal. Fortunately, he still had well over $1,000 in listings that were still active.

He'd also used up a lot of his $2,500 savings, which he'd transferred in full to his debit account. But he wasn't worried about that, because he figured the worst-case scenario was that he could sell the items back for close to the original price.

While he'd been out and about that morning, he'd thought about something else: *what about the time cost of money?* You didn't need a business degree to know that your time was worth something.

If he hadn't been scurrying around looking for camera lenses to buy, he could have been with Maya, or running on the track, or just playing video games. He'd exchanged those opportunities to work on his "assignment"—so what was his hourly wage as a trainee?

Adding it up as well as he could, he figured that so far he was earning roughly $25 an hour in his new reselling life. Not bad, but not amazing. The consultant in him knew that even if that number sounded good, the lack of benefits and other disadvantages of being a full-time textbook reseller were significant drawbacks.

By applying his Brightside brain, however, he also realized another important fact. That number was an average of the time he'd spent so far, *but some hours were far more profitable than others.* For example, when he hit the jackpot of lenses at the estate sale, the hour he would spend taking photos, writing a description, and ultimately shipping them to a buyer was worth at least $100.

Not only that, but he also realized that a lot of his time had been spent *learning.* It took more than an hour to type up his notes from meeting with Clarence, but it was worth it because restating the material in his own words led to greater retention. The whole time he was learning and then studying, he wasn't making any money at all—but it had the potential to be highly valuable.

He shouldn't factor his learning time into his hourly wage, Jake realized. He only had to learn a lesson once, and then it would help him make future decisions. If he subtracted the learning time from the calculation, his profits were much better—more like $40 to $50 an hour.

Before he logged off for the night, he did some more calculations to see where he was at overall. Adding it all up, he came up with a current total of $645.20. He still needed $355 to complete the assignment, and he only had a few more days—but if his auctions inched higher, he'd get there.

It really was possible.

10.

FOR IMMEDIATE RELEASE
The Buzzard Takes Flight!

Emeryville, CA—Sharing your data with major corporations will become essential to improving your life, according to the founder of a new service that promises to change the way you make decisions.

The service, Buzzard, is now open in beta launch for a limited number of users.

"We're excited to swoop down and get this party started!" said Kevin Quan, the company's founder, CEO, and COO.

Quan founded the service as a way to "make data sharing sexy." By providing access to their email account, credit card statements, and other info, users will receive specific recommendations. They'll learn how to make better choices, including everything from what to wear to that big interview to what kind of partner they are most compatible with.

There is no cost to use the service. The company plans to partner with brands to offer personalized advertising campaigns, bringing valuable offers to users.

Contact:

Hilary Hodgkins

hils@buzzardco.com

1820 N. Woodson, Ste. 391

Emeryville, CA

Phone: +1-503-852-1465

From: Kevin Quan, Founder & CEO & COO

To: All Staff

Fellow Buzzers,

Today is an exciting day. It feels like only yesterday I was at Stanford, dreaming about starting a company and learning how to "nudge" people into making good choices—which is of course what Buzzard Co. is all about.

With the beta launch of our system, we'll bring better decisions to millions of people, while providing relevant (key word!) ads on behalf of our partners. And it all starts today!!

Join me in the new Buzz Lounge at 4:00 p.m. for tequila tasting. Last one there has to eat the worm . . .

Buzzing with anticipation,

Kevin

Secretive Startup Unfolds Its Wings

By Katlyn Everett

Valley News

Rumors have been flying for weeks about a new social platform, and today the service announced its beta launch. Buzzard Co., a Bay Area startup, promises to go where no social network has gone before—even though plenty have tried and ended up being sued by the government. But hey, pivot and relaunch, right?

Kevin Quan, the twenty-nine-year-old founder, promises that his company's proprietary algorithm can help you make decisions . . . and it's completely free. The catch? Users give up their data, and not just some of it. To make the most of the service, you need to hand over your email log-in, your bank statements, and even your browser history. Remember what you learned in basic econ, kids: there's no such thing as a free lunch.

The holy grail of personalized recommendations takes a while to kick in. "Don't worry, it's worth the wait!" says Quan, who is seeking investors following an initial round of funding from connections in Singapore.

If you'd like to sign away your life on an unproven service—and I mean, if you've tried online dating, it can't be worse—visit BuzzardCo.com/beta.

From: Kevin Quan, Founder & CEO & COO

To: Katlyn Everett, Valley News

Hi, Katlyn,

Thanks for featuring Buzzard in Valley News. I've been a fan for years!

I just wanted to pass on a few corrections to your story. I hope you can make these changes to the piece ASAP.

First, users won't "give up their data." It will be kept securely in the cloud, on a server that no one can access without a series of passwords. And don't worry, none of them will be "password1234"—I learned that lesson in college!

Second, to call the service "unproven" is a little unfair. Sure, we're new, but give us a chance and we'll PROVE it to you!

I'm including my cell phone number in case you ever need to reach me directly. Maybe we could grab a drink sometime?

———

From: Kevin Quan, Founder & CEO & COO
To: Katlyn Everett, Valley News

I see. No, I'd never tell you what to say in your reporting . . . just wanted you to have a little perspective from the 50,000-foot landscape where I spend most of my time when I'm not "down in the trenches."

And no problem about not wanting to meet up. Maybe another time!

Buzz off (j/k!),

Kevin

———

From: Zach Aarons, Buzzard Co. Marketing Team
To: All Staff

Hey, guys! I've been working with Kevin and the rest of the crew, and wanted to show you the process we're using for all the new users who are joining up today. We suggest using the phrase "Buzzard: Life Less Complicated" as a short catchphrase of what the service is all about.

We've also added a FAQ in response to several questions we've been getting. Take a few minutes before this afternoon's happy hour to familiarize yourself with it. It's important that we're all on the same page with these talking points.

To the Buzz,

Zach

Dept. of Marketing & Margaritas

Buzzard Co.
—Beta User Onboarding—

Thanks for signing up! Get ready to Buzz . . .

How It Works

1. You tell Buzzard everything about yourself. Don't worry, it's totally private! Your info will be used to help you make better decisions.

2. As the system learns more about you, it will begin to send you notifications on the most optimal life choices to make. Sit back and relax—you'll no longer have to worry about making so many decisions every day.

3. Over time, we plan to partner with relevant advertisers to bring you personalized content and valuable offers. These offers will help you level up!

That's all there is to it. Please note that Buzzard requires access to the following accounts:

- Email log-ins (personal, corporate, etc.)
- GPS data (automatically provided through your smart-phone)
- Three months of your most recent credit card statements
- Browser history, including any private windows or sessions

New! Frequently Answered Questions

Q: Why do you need so much information?
A: Because we want to help you! If the system doesn't know who you are, it can't really tell you the best decisions to make, can it?

Q: What kinds of decisions will Buzzard make for me?
A: You tell us! Or actually, we'll tell you—but you can choose from a range of decision-making power. Buzzard can help you with everything from deciding where to invest your retirement fund to who you should message on your preferred online dating service. We want to be there for you wherever you go!

Q: How much does this cost? Probably an arm and a leg, right?
A: Nope. Buzzard is FREE!! That's right, the cost is zero dollars. In fact, if you join now you might even end up *making* money once we open our referral program.

Q: How do I sign up??
A: Now we're talking! Just head to BuzzardCo.com/beta to get in before all your friends do. You don't want to be left out.

From: Kevin Quan, Founder & CEO & COO

To: Zach Aarons, Hilary Hodgkins

Awesome to see new users registering all day!

Where did our final numbers end up?? I'm going to try to generate more buzzzzz . . .

———

From: Kevin Quan, Founder & CEO & COO

To: Zach Aarons, Hilary Hodgkins

Cool . . . and yes, 3,000 new users is great. But I figure a lot more people will sign up tonight, so I might give a slightly higher number for media reports. On the phone with a journalist from Wall Street right now, wish me luck!

———

"This Just In" Evening Wrap-Up

Cheddar Media

New York—Shares of the Chinese toymaker Real Action spiked to $127 today, in response to strong demand for its line of reality show contestant action figures.

Rupert Howley, who pled guilty to the largest financial fraud scandal since Bernie Madoff, was released from prison after serving a sentence of three days.

In startup news, early reports suggest that the social service Buzzard signed up more than ten thousand users in its first day. Kevin Quan, founder, CEO, and COO, claims that the company is "blown away" by the response. "We knew we were on to something big, but this is truly buzzworthy!" he said.

The numbers could not be immediately verified.

11.

When Jake left the apartment on Monday morning, he knew his days there were numbered. By his count, he had less than two weeks left—an estimate that turned out to be overly optimistic.

Before he acquired that vital intelligence, he had to sit through another staff meeting between Brightside and the "transition team" from Magnate. These meetings were known as "team sharing," but the transfer of information was mostly one-way.

After the meeting kicked off, an HR manager appearing on a video feed began to explain the new assessment tool.

"You'll be measured on a variety of indicators," she told them, "but hours spent at the office and contribution to the bottom line are the most important."

The Brightside group watched from the conference room. "Everyone at Magnate is eager to bring on board the best-performing employees from our new West Coast office," she continued from afar.

Whatever pretense there had been about this not being a merger was ending. The next step in the "strategic partnership" was to begin the process of switching over to Magnate's branding. After they'd brought those best-performing employees on board, of course.

Marcie, the HR rep, kept going. "You won't know the precise algorithm, since it's all run by a computer, but the results will be shown throughout the company at each week's check-in meeting."

"When does it start?" Preena asked.

"Good question. It started a week ago." Marcie looked down at some notes. "Is Jake Aarons in the room?"

Jake thought about pretending to look around the room in search of another version of himself. But in the end, he reluctantly raised his hand. Jan was in the meeting, and he didn't want to make her life difficult.

Marcie got straight to the point. "Jake, you're at the bottom. The system dinged you for a low feedback score in the Avery Tech preso the other day. There's also a note about being late for our last team-sharing call between the two offices on Monday."

How did they even know about that? It's not like anyone was taking attendance.

He found his answer when he saw Sloan half disguising a smirk while he pretended to write something down.

Oh . . . right. He probably sent the tattletale email "out of concern for making sure everything goes smoothly in the transition."

———

Jake wasn't thrilled about starting from the bottom, and he didn't like his odds in any automated assessment process. But he also noticed a big change in how he felt today. Among other things, he worried less than he normally would have. Something about his recent experiment had changed him.

He knew it was a little silly. He hadn't even locked in the $1,000 yet. And what was he going to do—quit his promising job in management consulting to sell textbooks for the rest of his life?

Yet there was something about the whole exercise that felt highly satisfying. He noticed it was affecting his confidence in other areas. During the meeting, he didn't even try to hide his eye-rolling when Sloan told Marcie how smart it was that they were doing the assessment.

All things considered, the day wasn't off to a bad start. At least until the phone rang after lunch.

"Jake? It's Roland, from Syndicate Leasing. Are you at the apartment? We're getting reports of a burst pipe in the unit above yours."

Not only was Jake not at the apartment, he was also tied up on an urgent client deadline. It would be another hour until he could dash out to the parking lot and speed home to check. When he did, it was even worse than he feared. His bathroom floor was flooded, with two inches of water seeping into the carpet in the hall.

There wasn't much he could do at that point. The master water controls had been turned off, so the flood had stopped—but it was clear that the floors throughout the unit would have significant damage.

He spent the next hour trying to mop up as well as he could. It was a futile effort. The apartment needed a cleaning crew for the immediate disaster, and then a contractor to repair the damage. As for Jake, he needed a raincoat.

Roland came by to take a look, grimacing when he saw the scene. "You have renter's insurance, right?" he asked. "In these situations they'll usually hook you up with a hotel room for at least a week."

Jake had a sinking feeling in his stomach. He remembered initialing the part of the lease that said he was required to maintain at least $10,000 in coverage. Then he remembered looking up a policy online, where it seemed simple enough to sign up. And then he remembered thinking, "I'll worry about that later."

Just like with the loans. Good one, Jake.

"Uh, yeah, I think so—I'll have to look it up," he finally said.

"Do you at least have someplace to stay tonight?" Roland asked.

Not your problem, Roland.

"I'll figure something out, thanks."

Roland left and Jake stood in the hall of his soggy apartment. He thought about calling Maya, but he felt even more discouraged about their relationship than before. There was no way he was going to get her involved with his problems. They were supposed to have dinner that night, but he sent her a message asking if they could push it to the weekend. Her reply seemed colder than usual: "Sure, okay. Talk to you later."

Then he packed up as much stuff as he could and headed for the Mazda. He drove to the gym parking lot and pulled into a spot away from the overhead lights.

Looking around, he saw all the amenities he could hope for. There was the twenty-four-hour gym, equipped with free bath-rooms and showers. A gas station on the corner offered a wide range of processed foods that looked like they could survive the apocalypse. Finally, as a special feature, he had the open sky for a roof instead of a more traditional ceiling. Ceilings were overrated, he decided.

Every once in a while, trucks pulled into the parking lot en route to the gas station, revving their engines each time.

Look on the bright side. It's like going to a hotel, just without a room. Or like camping, without all the peace and quiet.

12.

When you spend the night in your car, you learn to adjust some basic expectations about comfort and safety. Jake settled in and was surprised how quickly he fell asleep. He was less surprised by the number of times he woke up.

Around midnight, he heard the sound of an approaching siren. For a moment he thought the police were coming to arrest him—for what, he wasn't sure—but finally a fire engine passed by his car and kept going. It took him half an hour to get back to sleep.

Sometime close to two a.m., a man shuffled by with a shopping cart full of bottles and cans that rattled with every cycle of the wheels.

From four o'clock onward, a cat howled, over and over.

Best as he could figure, Jake had managed about four hours' sleep at most. At five a.m. he rolled out of bed, a.k.a. the backseat of the Mazda, and stretched. If he was making a gratitude list, item number one was that he lived in the mild climate of Southern California. Things could always be worse—as he'd learned by now.

One more thing on the list: his gym was close to the Lava Java. Before he'd been sidetracked by the burst pipe, he'd emailed Clarence to ask if he could meet again. In his reply, Clarence said he was going on a short trip, but if they could meet even earlier than the last time, they'd have at least twenty minutes until he had to leave for the airport.

Jake grabbed a shower at the gym and drove the few blocks to the coffee shop. This time, Clarence was the only one in the place. The owner hadn't shown up yet, but apparently he'd left a key for his favorite customer.

Clarence had already prepared the coffee and was waiting for his student. Did this guy ever take a break?

"Good morning, Jake! Do you have any used textbooks I can buy?"

Jake laughed. "As a matter of fact, I do—but they're going quickly."

They took a seat and Jake opened his notebook.

"Hey, Clarence," he said, "before we start, I just want to say how much I appreciate your time. I don't know what the final outcome of all of this will be, but it's making a real difference in my life."

He told him about the reselling experiment and mentioned how he felt significantly better even though the profit was still relatively small.

"I'm happy to do it, Jake," said Clarence. "And what you're

talking about is an important milestone. You're feeling better because you're starting to see what's possible. Remember, the most important thing I could ever tell you is—"

"—I need to start drinking better coffee?"

"Well, yes. That, too! But I was thinking of the Third Way philosophy: *you can do more than you think.* By learning how to buy and sell those textbooks, you're learning that you're not powerless. In the worst-case scenario, you could do that all the time and be able to pay your bills."

"Awesome. Well, I know we don't have much time," Jake said. "So I made a list of questions. How can I go from the $1,000 challenge to having a real business? Should I try to specialize or sell some of everything? And how do I keep track of it all if I have even more auctions? I imagine that it could start to get out of control."

"Those are all good questions," said Clarence. "But since our time is short, I have a different idea. Or to be precise, I have a new assignment for you."

He went on. "You're absolutely right that there's a lot more to learn about reselling. We could talk about drop-shipping, where you don't keep any inventory on hand, allowing you to operate the business remotely. We could talk about how to find more items to sell. We could talk about tools and resources to make the whole process more efficient. But the fact is that you can learn all of that on your own."

Jake made a note to add drop-shipping to his list of topics to research further.

"Okay," he said when he looked up. "So I'll try to learn more about that before we meet up again. But you said you have a different assignment?"

"Uh-huh," said Clarence. "So there's good news and bad news. You already heard the good news: you've learned a very important skill. Bad news is . . ."

Jake waited. He was learning that Clarence liked to be dramatic with these things.

". . . Bad news is, it's not enough. Think it through and follow it to its logical end. Where does it leave you? Do you want to be buying and selling textbooks for the rest of your life?"

For a few months, sure. For the rest of my life . . . probably not.

"And the other question you have to answer is, does it pass the grandparent test?"

"The grandparent test?"

"Yeah. Jake, do you still have grandparents around?"

He did, or at least he had two of them. He was especially close to Grandma Norris on his mom's side. Approaching ninety, she still had a lot of spunk and a quick wit.

Clarence explained that the grandparent test consisted of a two-part question. First, when you think about your business, can you easily explain it to your grandparents? If your answer is, 'Well, it's complicated . . .' then you've already failed the test. Second, if it seems like it's understandable enough, would you be comfortable telling them about it?

Jake wrote "grandparent test" on a new line of his notebook.

"Let me give you an example," Clarence explained. "A while

back I worked with a guy who was really good at the reselling thing. He started just like you, and within a year or so, he was making a lot of money. So far, so good, right?"

Jake waited.

"Over time he began to specialize, and one of the markets that he became an expert in was, well, let's call it the market of consenting adults. Basically, he learned how to buy boxes of condoms at a discount from a manufacturer and resell them to stores around the country."

He waited again.

"So, Jake, there's nothing wrong with selling condoms . . . but would you want to tell your grandparents about it?"

Jake burst out laughing at the idea of telling Grandma Norris that he had become a professional condom reseller. He'd sooner crawl under the table and starve at a holiday dinner than have that conversation.

Clarence went on. "Forget about that example for a moment, because it's not just about the specific items. With *any* reselling category, all you're doing is marking up the price of something. You're only profiting because the system is inefficient. Economists call this 'rent-seeking,' which is a fancy way of saying you're not really adding anything of value.

"Making money is good, for all the reasons we've talked about. But ultimately, you should learn to make money while also helping people in a meaningful way. That's what the test is about. Don't you want your grandma to be proud of you?

"She's your grandma, so chances are she'll always be proud of you no matter what you do. But wouldn't *you* feel better if you could tell her about all the people you were helping with your work?"

Jake thought about what Maya was doing in her work with the nonprofit that served newly settled immigrants. There was no doubt that she was making a difference in the world. As for him, he liked working with businesses and didn't think he should quit his job and work for a charity. After all, charities need to get their funding from somewhere. Was there some way he could use his skills to make a difference *while* making money at the same time?

Clarence had taken a short break to respond to a message on his phone. Now he looked back up.

"Alright, enough with the grandparent test—you get it. There's another very important reason why you need to go beyond reselling. Right now you don't really have any sort of passive income."

Jake had never heard of retail arbitrage, the phrase that Preena had mentioned the other day, but he was familiar with the promise of passive income. The phrase had become a bit of a cliché. Once, while browsing at a bookstore, he'd spent an hour leafing through a whole shelf of books that promised such a thing. Most of them seemed to suggest that readers buy the author's course on acquiring real estate properties. When he mentioned this, Clarence immediately became animated.

"I'm glad you brought that up! Buying rental properties is one small field of passive income," he said, "and it's not realistic for most people. Here's another test, and this one's easier. Do you have enough money for a down payment on a bunch of old houses or apartments?"

"Nope." *That was an easy question.*

"And do you have enough time to wait years, maybe even a decade or longer, to 'build your portfolio' like those guys talk about?"

"Definitely not." *Also easy.*

"Last but not least, do you even *want* to be a landlord?"

Jake thought about his recent experience dealing with the burst pipe. "It doesn't sound very attractive."

"Right. Buying rental properties works for a small number of people—and good for them—but most folks should look elsewhere. I should put this on a bumper sticker. *Passive income: it's not just about real estate.*

"Here's what's far more obtainable. Imagine waking up to a notification that says there is more money in your bank account than there was when you went to sleep. Anything that gets you closer to that point is your goal."

That sounded good to Jake. What sounded even better, at least at the moment, was the idea of sneaking away somewhere to take a nap. He shook it off and forced himself to focus. If he could figure this out, he knew he'd be much better off.

———

Clarence had almost finished his coffee. "Alright, we just have a few minutes left, so let's cut to the chase. The shortest path to passive income is to offer some kind of service that people can pay for. Therefore, your new assignment is to create your first service. This is something that you do for someone else, not something you buy and then resell. It's also different from making your own products for sale, which is also a good approach, but one that will take a bit longer."

"Okay," Jake said while taking notes. "But that still sounds like work, not just cashing checks that show up without me doing anything."

"It's the first step of a process," Clarence replied. "In this version, yes, there's still work to be done. But it's a logical place for most people to start, and you can nurture it into something more fully passive once you have a customer base."

He then explained that Jake's new service business had to meet a few conditions:

1. It had to pass both parts of the grandparent test.
2. It had to accommodate the obligations of his day job.
3. This time, he couldn't spend *any money* at all. It needed to be a true $0 startup.

"One thing I can't stress enough: be careful not to overcomplicate it. A lot of people get hung up on 'thinking big.' They have the idea that they're supposed to be like Steve Jobs or some other famous entrepreneur. A better way for most of us is to think very, very simple. What can you do that people will pay you for? How

can you use what you've learned to help people with something—
and help them enough that they'll gladly exchange money for it?

"And one more thing: think *specific*. Another mistake people
make is trying to do something too general or too broad.

"Alright, I have to get to the airport." He looked at his phone
again and requested a car to pick him up outside. "I'll be in Seattle
and out of touch for the next couple days, so let's plan on connecting at the group meeting on Thursday."

Jake had been making more notes the whole time. "But wait,"
he said as Clarence was leaving. "How do I know what kind of
service—"

"Right, that's exactly what you need to answer."

13.

Back in high school, Jake had boarded the bus one day and realized he'd forgotten the six-page term paper that was due later that morning. To be precise, he hadn't just forgotten to bring it. He'd forgotten to *write* it.

He'd known about the assignment for weeks, but sometimes knowledge was more of an obstacle than an advantage. Give him a short deadline and he'd knock it out with time to spare, but give him all the time in the world and it would never happen.

Still, this was a *very* short deadline. The only good news was that his English class wasn't until fourth period. Jake didn't learn much in chemistry that morning, and he didn't learn anything at all in Spanish—a fact he'd later regret after meeting Maya. He used the time to work at a desk in the back of the room, handwriting a cogent argument about *Great Expectations*. His argument included references to two other books by Dickens, as well as several modern-day hip-hop quotes.

Third period was programming class, where Jake had temporary access to a computer he could use to type up his notes. He'd worry about the code he was supposed to be writing later. One of his friends was in the lab right before Jake went to English class, and he helped out by performing a quick spell-check, pumping up the font size and maximizing the margins to get from four and a half pages to six, and printing it out.

Jake handed over his morning masterpiece in the nick of time, feeling exhausted and proud. The best part of all was when Mr. Michaels returned the paper a week later. His grade was an A minus, with minor points taken off for grammar and only one complaint about the font being too big. He even made a passing comment in front of the class that Jake's friends found hilarious: "I can tell you spent some real time on this, Jake."

Mr. Michaels went on to say that he especially liked how Jake contrasted the conflict between Pip and Miss Havisham in relation to the current "rapper feud" between DJ Silver Kittens and Li'l Bazooka. After that, Jake felt invincible the rest of the semester.

And that was how he felt this morning, more than a decade later—at least at first.

He was already thinking about what his new service business would be. An idea was percolating in the back of his mind, and as soon as he had more time after sorting out his housing situation, he'd start working on it.

There was something strangely comforting about being in debt, sleep deprived, in trouble at work, and even temporarily home-less . . . yet still feeling positive. His time with Clarence had been encouraging. Like he'd said that morning, he didn't know how it would all turn out, but he felt significantly better about his prospects.

That was why he was so unprepared for what came next.

He'd skipped dinner with Maya the night before, not wanting to explain that she now had a boyfriend who lived in a car. He fig-ured she was busy after her trip to Denver while he'd been hunting camera lenses at yard sales. That morning when he'd left the Lava Java, he meant to call her, but ended up thinking about ideas for his new service on the way into work. Once he arrived at the of-fice, there was the usual client work waiting for him.

That day she'd called a couple of times when he was in meet-ings. Each time he made a mental note to call her back, but then forgot. He'd need to make it up to her soon, maybe even with a return visit to the Thankful Bistro—one that he could afford to pay for.

Now he saw he had a message from her in his personal inbox, the one he'd been avoiding ever since getting his eviction notice and loan collection request on the same day.

But he couldn't avoid this message. It was titled, simply, "Us."

From: Maya Alvarez

To: Jake Aarons

Hey Jake,

I didn't want to do this by email, but I tried to call you a couple times today and you didn't call back. Plus, what happened with dinner last night?

Listen—I know you're busy and going through some stuff. But it also seems that you don't have time for a relationship right now, or at least the relationship that I want to have. I like you a lot, but maybe the time isn't right for us. I'd like to take a break and figure out what's best for me.

I think I have your Cal State sweatshirt and a couple of other things. I can bring them by your place sometime next week.

A sinking feeling came over him as he read and reread the note. He immediately picked up the phone to call her, ignoring a conference call he was supposed to be monitoring on the other line. The call went straight to voice mail. He called back five minutes later and the same thing happened.

"Maya, I'm sorry," he wrote in a text. "You're totally right and I haven't done a great job explaining some things lately. Can we talk?"

He could see that she'd read the message right away. But although Jake spent the better part of the evening staring at the phone, telepathically communicating that he really could do a better job, he never got a reply.

Act II

14.

Buzzard Launches Referral Program

Emeryville, CA—The social network everyone's talking about is getting ready to invite a huge new wave of users into the hive.

"Buzzard promises to pay you back for all those hours you've wasted by scrolling through photos online," says Kevin Quan, the company's founder, CEO, and COO. "Now you can waste your friends' time . . . and earn BuzzBucks™!"

The company's referral program, launching today, offers power users a chance to get paid. These "honeypots," as they'll be known, will earn up to $50 for every new user they recruit.

Interested? Check your email for more info . . . your friends might already be recruiting you!

Contact:

Hilary Hodgkins

hils@buzzardco.com

1820 N. Woodson, Ste. 391

Emeryville, CA

Phone: +1-503-852-1465

———

From: Kevin Quan
To: All Staff

What a great first week it's been! People are loving Buzzard!!

In other news, I want to apologize for my behavior at last week's tequila tasting. With all the excitement over our launch, I guess I got a little too buzzed up!

As part of our efforts to maintain a productive workplace, HR has asked that we restrict the consumption of hard liquor until after 5:00 p.m. I have grudgingly agreed to this request, as long as our special microbrew station is allowed to remain open for lunch. We can't let them ruin *all* the fun.

Also, as most of you know, today we're launching the referral program. I think it's really gonna pop!

Remain alert,

Kevin

(Still CEO & COO)

———

From: Kevin Quan

To: HR

No, I'm not worried at all. I don't think the term "honeypot" suggests anything other than "let's make some money!"

Personally, I think we could all stand to be a little less politically correct around here . . .

———

From: Kevin Quan

To: Our Awesome Users

Buzzzzzzz!

I hope you're having a great day! As your Chief Buzzard, I wanted to let you know that our referral program is live! You're now able to get paid by recruiting your friends to join the hive.

How will you get paid, you ask? You can use our new currency, BuzzBucks™, in the online store found directly in the app! And that's not all—BuzzBucks™ can also be exchanged for *real cash money* through a simple conversion process—though I think most of you would rather be sporting the latest in BuzzMerch. ;)

All you need to do to get earning is email your friends, and we've made that part easy. Since we already have access to your address book, you can just click a button indicating your approval for us to email them on your behalf.

We'll automatically include your referral link, so when they sign up, you'll get paid!

To the Buzz,

Kevin Quan

Founder & CEO & COO

"Buzzard Co. promises to go where no social network has gone before." —Valley News

---

Buzzard Puts the Pyramid Back in the Scheme

By Katlyn Everett

Valley News

Pop Quiz: What does the term "honeypot" refer to?

- A) A slang word for vagina
- B) An attractive woman used as bait to recruit spies around the world (so in other words, "A")
- C) The latest lame marketing scheme from Buzzard, the social service that your friends keep spamming you about

Time's up! If you guessed "D," all of the above, you win a free referral worth $50. Or so claims Kevin Quan, the founder ("and CEO and COO") of Buzzard.

After debuting with more of a flutter than a buzz last week, the social network that makes your decisions (as long as you give them all your data) today announced a referral program like no other. With a click of a button, the service will—wait for it—spam every one of your contacts with invitations to "join the hive."

You'll also get paid "up to $50," though the details of the service's newly invented currency are unclear. You're probably asking yourself: Isn't this illegal? If it's not, shouldn't it be?

That said, here's an idea. If you really want to join up, head over to Buz zardCo.com/referral and use my referral code, "Pyramid." All proceeds earned from these referrals will be donated to the Electronic Protection Foundation, which works to protect the personal data of individuals from corporate overreach.

———

From: Kevin Quan
To: Katlyn Everett
Katlyn, I would appreciate you calling me for comment prior to publishing these articles. They really are below the reputation of a long-standing establishment such as the Valley News.

However, in the spirit of compromise, I'm happy to let bygones be bygones. We'll even put 200 extra BuzzBucks™ in your account. Cha-ching! And if you change your mind about that drink sometime . . . give me a buzz! (Get it??)

Kevin Quan

Founder & CEO & COO

"Buzzard Co. promises to go where no social network has gone before." —Valley News

———

From: Kevin Quan
To: Katlyn Everett
Hi Katlyn. Just wanted to make sure you got my last message?

———

From: Kevin Quan

To: Zach Aarons, Hilary Hodgkins

Hilary, I know I changed the announcement a little before it went out—sorry if I caused any trouble. I just thought it would be good to add a dollar amount to be more specific.

BTW, can one of you look at how we can convert the referral incentives to cash?

I think I said that we'd pay them up to $50 for every new user . . . we can do that, right? I'm hoping for a big round of investment soon.

———

From: Kevin Quan

To: Our Awesome Users

Buzzzzzzz!

Just a quick clarification on the referral program. We didn't expect so many of you to jump on it so quickly! We're going to do what we can to make those payments to everyone who has already notched up so many new accounts.

However, I'd encourage you to adopt a new motto: *refer responsibly.* We want new users, but it doesn't help when all of them turn off the data-sharing options. We can't get paid without that!

Going forward, we're going to restrict the $50 credit for use in the BuzzBucks™ online store, NOT in conversion to money like I first said. Fail fast, right? We have to keep the lights on over here!

Kevin Quan

Founder & CEO & COO

———

From: Kevin Quan

To: Social Media Team

I heard that you guys are taking a lot of flak from people online. Remember the first rule of the internet: never read the comments section . . . but now that I think about it, I guess that's your job. Ha!

Here's an idea. What if we create a special "Buzz Badge" that people can use for their social profiles? We'll call it "show the world your Buzz pride!"

I was just reading a study about how millennials are more motivated by recognition than money. Maybe if we recognize them, they'll forget about the payments.

Thoughts??

———

From: Kevin Quan

To: Investors

CONFIDENTIAL

Hi everyone, I wanted to quickly report in from the trenches.

Everything is going much better than I hoped! I'm expecting massive growth and a bunch of big partnerships to be signed soon.

We just have one problem: cash flow. Because of a new referral program, we owe some of our more active users a lot more money than we expected.

I'll be speaking with the person who was in charge of setting this up, to make sure it never happens again. But in the meantime, we really need an influx of new funds. Any ideas??

15.

The rest of the night had been a blur. Jake had called Maya repeatedly, before he backed off and texted to say he'd give her the space she wanted. He was smart enough to know not to overdo it. He also knew he shouldn't give up, but for now he needed to put his immediate attention elsewhere.

Wednesday morning, he went back to the track and pounded out his six miles. The Third Way group was meeting the next day, and he wanted to have his new service ready to go. And, of course, he was still responding to inquiries from his online auctions and getting ready to ship out a bunch of books to new buyers.

After work, when he wasn't thinking about Maya and trying not to stalk her social media accounts, he'd been thinking about what the service should be. Back in college, he'd taken a workshop on negotiation. It was a short class that met only once a week for four weeks, but it made a lasting impact. He liked the idea of gaining an advantage for yourself while also making the other party feel like they weren't losing.

Maybe this was something he could help people with. He could even picture a tagline: *The Art of Negotiation, by Jake Aarons.*

There was another small matter to overcome: based on his recent track record at Brightside, he wasn't actually that good at what he proposed to teach. But he figured that hadn't stopped him before. He could learn as he went along, right?

He knew he'd need to create a specific offer, like Clarence said. In his marketing work, he'd learned to craft a pitch based on the benefit the customer would receive. Focus on that ultimate promise, he remembered, not the list of features or details.

The first promise he thought of was short and sweet: "Become a better negotiator."

Then he thought a bit more. His next idea added a clearer outcome: "Become a better negotiator in ten easy steps."

That was an improvement, but ten steps sounded like a lot. He settled on a modification: "Become a better negotiator in six easy steps."

Great. Those four extra steps were highly overrated.

There was still something about it that didn't feel right, but Jake decided to ignore the feeling for now. He had to move forward.

Next, he needed a website.

The Third Way group was big on getting things done quickly, so when it came to making his site, he followed their model. Looking at the resources mentioned in the manifesto Clarence had sent, he found step-by-step instructions for getting it set up.

His first task was to expand upon that headline. "Become a better negotiator in six easy steps" was a good start, but he needed more. What problem was he trying to solve? He took a stab at writing a full paragraph:

Are you trying to negotiate a pay raise, a day of working remotely, or anything else from your employer? You need to learn the essentials of negotiation! In this action-packed coaching session, I'll give you six easy steps that will help you get more of what you really want.

That sounded better. Then he wrote two more paragraphs, trying to make the connection between improving negotiating skills and feeling better about yourself.

The Third Way model also suggested providing an explanation of why you were qualified to provide the service. Jake puzzled over that one for a while. "I took a short class in college and now I'm an expert, even though I can't seem to apply what I learned to myself" didn't sound promising.

He tried a different approach, following the model he'd used for his first paragraph. "I started working as a negotiation consultant because I wanted to help people get more of what they really want."

Not bad.

He kept going. The next part of the model suggested he write a "call to action," or CTA. The CTA should tell people what they'll get when they hire you, and then urge them to do so.

Jake wrote:

> When you sign up for a session with me, you'll learn six easy ways to improve any negotiation. Click here to get started!

Jake looked at it. "Click here to get started" wasn't going to win any copywriting awards, but it clearly communicated the message. He linked that sentence to his online bank account. When users clicked it, it gave them the option to pay right away using their credit or debit card.

As for pricing, he decided on a flat rate of $250 per consultation. He figured he'd spend an hour or two talking with a client, then write up a list of recommendations. Maybe he'd follow up a couple weeks later to see how they were doing.

At the end of the evening, he had his simple, one-page website. He had a description of his services. He had a way for clients to sign up. Done!

And now, the money would start rolling in. Right?

16.

If the negotiation service actually worked, it would be amazing. By the time he'd decided on the price, he was already doing the math in his head. *If I have three clients per week and charge $250 for the consultations . . . that's an extra $3,000 a month.*

Combined with his salary, that kind of money would allow him to get another nice apartment *and* start paying down those loans. Or he could look for a cheap studio and focus even more on getting out of debt, thus freeing him up to do something bigger and better in a year or two. Could it really be that easy?

He'd heard Preena tell a story about Paul, another group member she'd met when she first started going. Paul had been selling virtual golf lessons for a while, and when he launched a new

"Putting Under Pressure" course, he watched the orders flood in as soon as the sign-up page went live.

Thinking of that story, and thinking about what an extra $3,000 a month would feel like, he flipped the switch that made his new website live.

What happens next?

The Third Way model suggested he tell all of his friends about the new project. Chances are, the theory went, someone you know can help you connect with your first buyers. He composed an email and social media post.

> Hey, everyone! I'm trying something new. If you've ever wanted to become a better negotiator, this might be good for you. If not, pass it on to someone else who might need it.

Then he sat back and waited.

Well, it's not going to be instant . . . might as well get back to work.

———

Being distracted at work was now the rule instead of the exception. First, there was the fact that he was sleeping in the Mazda. Then there was the reality that he'd had more than a few unexpected events in his life recently.

The office itself was in a strange sort of flux. With the introduction of the new assessment tool, everyone seemed to be adjusting their behavior to fit whatever they thought it was measuring. Preena was turning in a flurry of memos, spacing them out instead of putting everything in a single, consolidated report. Sloan was emailing the rest of the office at six a.m., then sending annoying follow-up messages if he didn't get a response within half an hour.

Even Jan seemed off her rhythm. More than once, she forgot that she'd scheduled an additional meeting, and then looked puzzled whenever the team walked into her office at the appointed time.

It was hard to know what to do.

The office gossip centered around the CEO of Magnate, effectively the boss of Brightside, who would be paying them a visit soon. They were told to expect key decisions to be made during that time, and who knows, maybe they'd even be informed about some of them.

Jake spent some time writing a report, updating Jan, and messaging with Preena about her jewelry business. All the while, he was wondering how his new experiment was going.

He'd been keeping an eye on his phone throughout the afternoon. It wasn't exactly blowing up. He sold a camera lens and another accounting textbook—all good news, since he was now above $800 in profit, well on the way to his $1,000 goal. There was no movement on the new service, however, and it puzzled him. He wasn't expecting a miracle, but he was expecting *something*. Instead, nothing happened.

A couple people had "liked" his post on social media. But the overall reaction was strangely muted. It wasn't that anyone hated it; it was that no one appeared to care.

Weird—maybe something was wrong with his notifications?

Was the site not working? When no one was looking, he made a test purchase, thinking that maybe he'd messed something up when linking his bank account. He probably should have done that sooner, but everything worked fine.

Good news: I just made $250. Bad news: it came from my own bank account.

At the end of the afternoon, he logged out and got ready for the weekly meeting with the Third Way group. From there he'd have another night of eating at Raul's before parking in the gym lot for his next attempt at sleep.

So far it looked like his first experiment was a bust. Maybe he should just focus more on selling textbooks.

He was missing something important, but he didn't know what it was.

17.

L adies and gentlemen, I'd like to introduce you to another newcomer. Tonight's special guest came all the way from Honduras!"

Clarence was presiding over the introduction to Jake's second meeting with the Third Way group. The special guest arrived in the form of dark beans that filled a small burlap sack. As people arrived and got settled, Clarence set up an elaborate coffee bar on the long table. He poured small cups and passed them out to murmurs of approval.

"I'll never think about coffee the same way," Adrian said by way of appreciation. Jake was planning to skip the special brew tonight—sleeping in the car was hard enough without being caffeinated—but found he couldn't resist taking a cup.

Clarence addressed the group. "Alright, listen up, everyone. Our other guest from last week, and I don't mean the Indonesian one, has an update for us. Jake, can you fill us in?"

Jake sat up. "Sure, of course. And thanks again for being so welcoming. I'm not sleeping much, and some other things haven't been going well . . . but I've also learned a lot about making money in a new way. Clarence gave me an assignment to make $1,000 before I saw you guys next. He didn't tell me how to do it—"

The group exchanged looks. Apparently this was typical of Clarence. He'd tell you what you needed to do, but you had to figure out your own way of doing it.

"—and after doing some research, I ended up buying a bunch of textbooks to resell. Then I went out over the weekend and bought some more stuff at yard sales. Long story short, this afternoon I crossed over the $1,000 goal."

The group cheered. "That's fantastic!" said Clarence. "It's definitely something to celebrate. You can build a solid side income just by buying and selling exactly like you've done. It's something that anyone can learn, and a lot of people should.

"But," he continued. "That was the first assignment. I also gave you—"

"Right." Jake was impatient. "A second assignment. That's what I wanted to get feedback on. Unfortunately, that one hasn't worked so well. Something isn't right, but I don't quite know what it is."

"Well, you've come to the right place," said Marta, the woman who was doing test-prep coaching. "Why don't you tell us more about what's going on?"

Jake filled them in on his grand idea to offer negotiation consultations. In his retelling, he noticed that it didn't sound as captivating as he'd thought it was the other day. He finished on a cliffhanger: "And so, I just thought more people would be interested, but so far . . ."

"Okay," said Clarence, finally. "I have some questions. But I bet other people do, too. Who's first?"

"Shouldn't we tell Jake the rule about feedback?" Celia had arrived late, but got settled just in time to hear the second part of his update.

"Yep," said Adrian. "It's pretty simple. Basically, we can't help you very much if we sugarcoat our feedback. We have to tell you what we really think, or else you won't walk away with anything helpful."

"Sounds good," Jake said. "I can take it."

"I have a question," said Jo. "Who is this 'negotiation service' for?"

That was an easy question. He was expecting something tougher from her.

"Oh. Well, it's for people who want to, uh, learn to negotiate better."

"But what does that mean?"

"To negotiate? It means to go back and forth on some issue, and hopefully come to a satisfactory resolution—"

"I wasn't asking how the word 'negotiate' is defined in the dictionary," Jo pressed him. "What I want to know is, imagine I have no idea what your service is about. Tell me why I should care. Tell me why it matters."

All of a sudden, Jake could picture Jo as a Siberian labor camp guard. *Tell me vhy I should care. Vhy does it matter.* He looked to the rest of the group for support, but they were all staring straight at him, expecting a response.

"Oh, okay. Well, basically it will help you get a better outcome when you talk to your boss about a raise, or"—he wavered again—"or whatever else."

Great ending. All he needed to do was add "and stuff" to cap off his latest stellar presentation.

"Alright, so it sounds like it's for anyone who has a job," Clarence said, no doubt coming to his rescue. "Is that about right?"

"Well, yeah! And not just people with jobs, but, like I said, other kinds of negotiations. It's really open-ended."

"So in other words, all kinds of people could benefit from this. In fact, almost *everyone* could. Correct?"

Jake felt like he was walking into a trap, but he didn't see anywhere else to go.

"Yeah." There was a long pause. "Isn't that good?"

"Not at all," said Clarence. "In fact, it's more likely a sure sign that you won't get very far."

He stood up and paced back and forth on one side of the table.

"Jake, saying that your service is for everyone is almost always a mistake. If you're offering free money, then sure, the whole world is your market. But otherwise, you really need to tighten up. Trying to serve everyone will lead to you serving no one."

Clarence looked across the table. "Let's take an example. Consider what Jo is doing with her dollhouse business."

For a moment Jake pictured Jo in Siberia, pushing dollhouse furniture on Russian spies. *Vant to buy coffee table? It vill look nice by sofa.*

He snapped out of it and kept listening.

"Jo, who are your customers?" Clarence asked.

"That's easy," she said. "They are women like me who grew up playing with dollhouses. About half of them have children of their own, and the other half are adult collectors."

"Okay, great." Clarence was getting animated. "So here's the thing. All kinds of other people *could* end up buying from Jo. These days, most of us wouldn't tell our kids that only girls should play with dollhouses. Some boys might get into it, just like more and more girls are doing things they weren't usually encouraged to do when I was a kid."

Jake nodded while taking notes, and Clarence continued.

"Even so, it's fair to say that the majority of Jo's customers are women, and they divide further into two subgroups: the ones with kids of their own, and the adult collectors who just like to relive memories. We could go on and on. I bet most of Jo's customers

make a certain income and are highly represented in certain professions. We could probably predict how they vote in presidential
elections, and what their favorite TV shows are.

"But here's the point: even without getting into all those details,
we already know quite a lot. We know who Jo is trying to reach,
and we know who she's *not* trying to reach."

Clarence sat down. "Understanding your customer is critical.
Again, if you think that what you're making is for 'everyone,' your
odds of success are very low."

———

"Hey, can I say something?" Celia had her hand up. "I totally agree
with this line of feedback. Jake doesn't know who his service is for.
But I also don't think it's the whole problem."

She shifted in her chair to look at him. "To me, the problem of
not knowing who it's for is related to not knowing what the service really is. And that's connected to the bigger picture behind it.
What's that other question we sometimes ask?"

"Why are you qualified to provide this service?" Jo spoke up
again. She had no problem being direct.

"Yeah," said Celia. "What are your credentials, or how do you
present yourself as an expert on the topic?"

Thinking quickly, Jake decided it was wise to not mention he'd
taken a single workshop on negotiation that met only four times.

"You're right," he conceded. "I don't have a degree in this subject."

Clarence jumped back in. "That's not really the issue. Unless you're planning to practice medicine, you don't need a college degree to offer your service. But you still need to demonstrate qualifications."

"That's what I was getting at," said Celia. "If I'm your prospective client, I don't care where you went to school and whether or not they gave you a pretty piece of paper with your name on it. But I *do* want to know that I'll be in good hands if I hire you."

"It's called *authority*," Adrian said, summing up Celia's point. "Whenever you're selling a service, you need to demonstrate authority. It's basically a core competency: do you know enough to deliver this service well, and will your client be better off after having your consultation?"

This was a lot to take in, but Jake nodded while taking rapid-fire notes. He knew it would be important to think more about this later.

Clarence looked around. "Jake, here's what it comes down to. Is this service really the best one you could offer? Sure, you could probably go back and improve it. But before you get too far along, you might want to ask yourself if a different idea might be better."

With that, he turned to the rest of the group. "Okay, let's move on so we can hear from some other folks. Who's next?"

Jake gave his note-taking hand a rest while he listened to other updates. It was never fun to hear that your idea was flawed. At the same time, he understood the rule about only providing honest feedback. If he hadn't had the critique tonight, he would have kept floundering along, unsure of why it wasn't working.

Now he knew he needed to change direction. The group was right that his idea needed a lot of revision. But what would he try next?

18.

"Hey Jake, can you stay behind a second? There's something I wanted to ask you."

Clarence spoke while rinsing out coffee cups in the sink, something that the group always tried to do for him but rarely succeeded at. "And you, too, Preena."

When he finished wiping the last cup, he came over and sat with both of them.

"I don't mean to pry, but Preena told me a little about what's going on with you. I understand you no longer have plans for Thanksgiving weekend?"

It was true. Jake had hoped that Maya's "let's take a break" announcement didn't mean that the Thanksgiving family visit was off, but unfortunately it did. He reluctantly wished her a good trip and hoped that there would be another chance later.

This meant, of course, that he wouldn't get to try those tamales.

It also meant that he wasn't sure what to do that week. He'd already told his parents that he wouldn't be coming home for the holiday. To backtrack now would just reinforce his sense of failure. He also hadn't mentioned the breakup to them, or anything about his new mobile living situation. The longer he could avoid talking about those things, the better.

"Well, yeah," he finally said. "I thought I'd be visiting someone, but that plan is on hold at the moment. So I figured instead I'd spend a bunch of time hunting down more textbooks and camera gear to sell."

And instead of trying to make a good impression with my girlfriend's family, I'll be catching up on all the latest shows on my laptop.

Clarence smiled. "That's not a bad idea, but I have a better one. Remember how we talked about the best way to learn?"

"Yes," Jake said. "'The best way to learn is to start.' With the $1,000 challenge, I thought I understood the concept when we talked about it, but it wasn't until I did it that I *really* understood."

"Exactly. So here's the idea: Want to go on a trip with me? We'd have a lot of time to talk, and you might be able to see how all of this stuff works in the real world."

"Wow, that would be great! Are you heading up to Seattle again?"

Jake imagined visiting the Space Needle, or at least seeing it from the ground. They probably charged a ridiculous admission fee for tourists.

Clarence and Preena exchanged a look. "It's a bit farther than that. Have you ever been to Ethiopia?"

"You're joking, right?"

Clarence wasn't joking. "I know it's short notice, but it's also a short trip. If we go over the holiday week, you'll only miss two days of work."

When he finally realized Clarence was serious, Jake shook his head. "Wow, that sounds incredible, but unfortunately I couldn't do something like that. I'm not really in a place to pay for a big trip right now. I wouldn't even know how much it costs.

"And I'd want to pay my own way," he added quickly. "You've already done a lot for me."

"I think that's where I come in," said Preena. "This trip would be really good for you, and I have a way to help. Remember all those trips I did last year to facilitate meetings for the client in South Carolina?"

He remembered. Last year Preena had flown back and forth to Charleston at least five times. There wasn't a direct flight, so each time she had to connect in Dallas or Chicago. One time, the client had an emergency right after she left—so after returning to California, she got on a plane to go straight back the next day. Another time she got stuck in a Midwest blizzard and ended up being rerouted with a triple connection, slogging through multiple cities in a daze before finally getting home.

"I also remember you saying you never wanted to travel again," he said.

"Right! Well, the only good thing that came out of that—besides the client work, of course—was that I earned a lot of frequent flyer miles. In fact, I earned enough to go pretty much anywhere, at least if you don't mind a middle seat in the last row of the plane. I already called the airline, and it looks like we can get you on the same flight as Clarence. I guess there aren't a lot of people flying to Ethiopia for Thanksgiving."

"And I'm staying in a guesthouse that has an extra room," said Clarence, "so it won't cost me anything extra for you to be there. I have some meetings and other things to do for about half the time. The rest of the time, I'll show you around and introduce you to some friends of mine. Whenever I'm busy, you can work from the house or explore on your own."

Jake didn't know what to say. Two weeks ago, he would have shrugged off the offer as a crazy idea. Now it sounded like he would be crazy to turn it down. Still, the trip was coming up very soon, and Africa seemed like a million miles away.

There were a lot of reasons why it didn't make any sense at all for him to go.

What am I getting into? How can I back out gracefully?

"When do we leave?" he finally asked.

19.

E *thiopia*. He'd heard of it, of course, but he didn't know much about it. When he went to Europe with Zach in college, they'd spent hours poring over guidebooks, plotting their itinerary. Now he was getting on a plane to fly even farther, and he wasn't even sure he could find his destination on a map.

The idea of preparing to leave in a few days seemed overwhelming at first. But the more he thought about it, the more he realized it wasn't nearly as complicated as he'd imagined. He was already planning to take a day off, in addition to the two days Brightside gave everyone for the holiday. He'd need to speak to Jan about being away a bit longer, but he'd hardly taken any vacation at all since starting at Brightside back in January.

Otherwise, half his stuff was in the Mazda, which he could leave parked at the office. He had a passport, and thanks to Preena's generosity, he had a plane ticket. He'd be with Clarence much of the time, and at this point he trusted him completely. Because of his assignment, Jake now had an extra thousand dollars in his bank account. He also had a powerful skill he'd learned in a short period of time—the skill of reselling—and the feeling that he could easily improve it with time and effort.

Last but not least, the Third Way group had shown him something he'd been looking for without fully knowing it. To understand that other people felt like he did was a true revelation. To know that he could earn at least *some* amount of money whenever he needed was huge.

There was just one thing nagging at him—or at least, one thing apart from the situation with Maya, which was never far from his mind. He hoped that they'd get more of a chance to talk when he was back.

What bothered him was that while he'd completed the first assignment with flying colors, so far the second had proved elusive. His negotiation business never really got started. He'd been excited about it at first, but the lukewarm response and the group's critique made him take a step back. Clarence told him that in these situations, sometimes you had to "tweak the offer," which basically meant changing something about the copy, the headline, or the price. Other times, he said, it was better to start all over with a totally different approach.

Another good thing about the Third Way model was that it cost very little to abandon ship. Jake hadn't spent a single dollar so far. Even if he got a bit further along, any money he spent would be minimal. All he'd really lose was his time, and since he learned something with each experiment, it wasn't a total loss.

Compare that to the traditional model of starting a business, he thought, like the hypothetical mom-and-pop coffee shop he had talked about with Clarence. If you tried to open a storefront business and it didn't work, you'd have real costs to pay for the failed attempt. Alternatively, if you tried to launch a company using the startup model, like Zach was doing with the Buzzard team, you had a whole other set of problems: investors to placate, even higher operating costs than a coffee shop, and the need to scale quickly or go out of business. These pressing concerns could lead to making shortsighted decisions—like launching a big referral program without clearly thinking through how users would respond.

As he pondered his options, he remembered an exercise that Preena had shown him. They'd been taking their breaks together and talking through different concepts. She said that before she decided on making handmade jewelry, the group helped her brainstorm options. They started by making a list of all the things she was good at, with no limits or filters.

The list included professional skills, what she'd learned in college, and hobbies. From there, she was able to brainstorm further to come up with several different ideas. She finally settled on making handmade jewelry, specializing in a nautical theme since she'd always loved ships.

Jake decided to try the exercise himself. Upon reflection, he accepted the fact that he wasn't really an expert at negotiation—and just like the group had pointed out, it wasn't a specific enough topic anyway. So what else could it be?

Preena had mentioned that it was important to think about your "soft skills" in addition to whatever technical knowledge you had. In other words, if you were good at talking with people and making them feel comfortable, that's a soft skill—hard to measure, but still valuable.

Jake realized that one of the things he was best at was getting out of challenging situations using creative solutions. He also worked well under pressure, like when he wrote that term paper in three hours.

Maybe he should take that mindset and see how to apply it to his service business . . . preferably without writing any more term papers.

An idea was beginning to emerge. What had he just learned to do? He had learned a proven, consistent way to make money whenever he wanted. It wasn't perfect, and he still had more to learn, but it was legit.

Furthermore, *why* had he just learned to do it? This seemed important. He'd learned to buy and resell items because he was feeling massive financial pressure—an all-too-common problem for a lot of people these days, especially college graduates his age or a few years younger.

He kept thinking, sensing that he was on to something. He just had to figure it out before he left for the trip.

———

In the movie version of Jake's life, the answer would come to him in a dream. But instead it came to him as he banged his head against the desk. Hard.

The answer, funnily enough, was *student loans*. Not that he should go out and borrow more money. He was pretty sure that door was closed, and fine by him. He wanted to be free of debt forever.

No, the answer was found in the fact that student loan repayment was a *tremendous* problem for his generation. Without looking up any figures, he guessed that there were hundreds of thousands of college graduates saddled with debt, and a good portion of them—just like him—were struggling to pay it back.

In other words, there was a clear problem. There was also a clear demographic. Jake understood his ideal customer, because that person was a lot like him. At a young age, they'd signed papers and received a lot of money in return. Everyone else was doing it, and besides, what alternative did they have?

Most students took out loans with the understanding that one day they'd need to pay them back, but they didn't always have enough foresight to make wise decisions. Not only that, after graduation many of them hadn't landed jobs with good enough salaries, so they had the same problem Jake did a few weeks ago. Even if they stretched their budgets and gave up their lattes, they'd still be stuck.

Problem, check. Customers, check.

But what was the *solution*? First, he had to think about why he was able to present himself as an expert, one of the hang-ups with his previous idea. He didn't have a finance degree, but both Clarence and Celia had said that didn't matter. Besides, there were plenty of people out there with finance degrees who couldn't figure out how to repay their loans.

He got into this mess in the first place by not having a plan. Does failing to plan or making a mistake qualify you as being an expert?

No, but finding a way out of the mistake does.

It wasn't money smarts that was helping him get out of debt, it was street smarts and creativity. He thought about Romeo George, the guy selling the washers and dryers. Presumably he didn't have a PhD in appliance flipping, but he'd found his way out of a tight spot nonetheless.

He thought about all those infomercials for diet and exercise programs. "I was just like you," the announcer would say. "Until I tried WonderCleanse, and then the weight came off." Even if he never advanced beyond reselling textbooks and camera gear, Jake now had a credible path to paying off that massive debt. He'd been running through the numbers, and they looked promising. Without doing anything else, simply maintaining the current quota of items he bought and resold, he'd be able to pay off his loans in less than three years. It might be a slog at times, but it worked.

Problem, customers, *and* authority. Check.

His solution was twofold. First, he'd try to educate students on the front end, either before they took out loans or at least before they graduated. This way, he could help them make better choices and minimize their future liability.

Second—*and here's where the revenue part comes in,* he thought, in response to an imaginary question from Clarence—he'd help people his age who needed practical guidance on paying down existing debt. He'd show them a solution based on what he'd learned through reselling. With minimal knowledge, anyone could follow a similar course of action and end up with real money in their pocket. If they applied their earnings to getting out of debt, they'd see significant progress in a short amount of time.

He started writing down everything he needed to do. Reviewing the steps he'd taken for his ill-fated negotiation project, he came up with a list of decisions he needed to make and tasks he needed to complete.

Then, after glancing at the time on his computer, he reluctantly set aside the list. As much as he wanted to jump right in, he had to get back to work, or to what he was increasingly thinking of as his "day job." He'd never used that phrase before, because he'd never had reason to. If your day job is your only means of getting paid, you just have a job. But now he had something else he was going to build, at least as long as he could survive whatever came at him in the next few weeks.

Jake suddenly remembered that he'd hit his head against the desk ten minutes earlier. Hard.

Huh. I guess that's why I have a pounding headache now.

But his head would be fine, at least as much as it ever was. He'd take some ibuprofen later. For now, he forced himself to close his laptop and begin reviewing client files for a proposal that was due in less than an hour.

20.

If there was one thing he'd learned from Clarence, it was that the answers were out there somewhere. He just had to find them. If there were two things, the second was that coffee was a wonderful elixir. He filled a large French press and set it on his desk, next to a cup that Maya had given him when they went on a trip to Coronado Island.

Everyone else had left the office for the day. Jake had left, too, but only for dinner. Not having a place at home to work—since he didn't exactly have an ergonomic workstation in the Mazda—he decided that returning to his desk would be the best option for the task ahead. Here he'd have good Wi-Fi, access to a printer, and whatever snacks his colleagues had left lying around the break room.

He also had a deadline. The next morning, he was meeting Clarence for the ninety-minute drive to LAX. They had an overnight flight to Germany and would connect on to Ethiopia from there. He planned to work on his service while he was traveling, but he'd committed to having a basic version ready to go before he left.

The clock was ticking. With coffee, an idea, and that unmovable deadline, he got to work.

He liked his idea of helping graduates pay off their student loans, as well as advising young students about how to keep any borrowing to a minimum. It felt strong. But he wanted to make sure he thought it through before diving in this time.

Looking back at the manifesto Clarence had sent, he went through the five points in order. The first point, to use the skills you already have, seemed simple enough. In addition to his actual experience with learning to buy and resell items, this new service seemed to play to his other strengths as well. Learning to write term papers on extremely short notice, thinking differently . . . these were traits he'd acquired that he could lean on.

It was the second point, to go from an idea to an offer, that puzzled him at first. What's an offer? He'd asked Preena about it, and she explained that when a lot of people get their first business idea, they don't really think of how it appears to the person they ultimately hope to sell to. Instead of being an afterthought, the Third Way model suggested that you *begin* with it.

A good offer is always designed to appeal to its ideal customer.

For example, if you were selling educational toys, kids would be the ones using them—but they weren't the customers. *Parents* were the customers. Therefore, when you described the offer, you should think about what kind of messaging would most appeal to parents.

Jake thought about his ideal customer: someone a few years out of school, like him, who had an average salary but was faced with repaying a large amount of money. His idea was to help that person . . . but how, exactly, would he do that?

He pulled out his notebook and began writing down potential approaches, starting with the benefit to the customer. The benefit was that if he could show people how to repay even a small portion of their loans, it would make a meaningful difference to them.

Not only that, he realized, but when a person is in debt, they often feel anxious and powerless. It's one thing to owe a lot of money, but it's another to *have no idea how you're going to pay it back*. If he could relieve some of that anxiety for his future clients, he knew it would be valuable.

He already had an idea in mind for a name: Student Loan Champion. It was a concept that had multiple meanings, and he pictured a comically exaggerated logo with a superhero holding a bag of cash over his head.

Now he needed a headline, a summary paragraph, and a call to action—a CTA. He started with something simple and straightforward: "Pay off your student debt."

That was his idea in a nutshell—but should the headline communicate anything else?

Debt, he knew all too well, is a burden. It contributes to worry, and sometimes even fear. Thinking about that in the context of his own experience, he added a couple of lines that addressed both points.

> *Worried about your student debt? I've been there. If you're willing to work hard, there's a skill you can learn that will take months or even years off your payments.*

He liked the last part ("there's a skill you can learn") because it offered hope to someone feeling burdened by debt. He also liked the qualifier ("if you're willing to work hard") because he only wanted to work with people who took it seriously. But what should his CTA be?

He went for something simple again.

> *Stop worrying and start breaking free of that burden. My consultation costs $150 and is fully guaranteed. If you don't agree that the skill you'll learn can make a real difference, you'll get another session free or your money back—your choice.*

Adding the guarantee was a bold move, but Jake felt confident he could deliver. Besides, in the unlikely event he couldn't help someone, he'd feel bad about taking their money when they were already experiencing hardship.

With his offer and website copy outlined, he was ready for stage two, setting up the site and all the tools he needed. He refilled his coffee and took a walk around the office.

Scrounging in the break room, he found some stale donuts. Sustenance! Zach had shown him the trick to restoring any day-old donut back to its delicious state of origin: ten seconds in the microwave, no more, no less.

If Student Loan Champion didn't work out, he'd consider making an app to teach people the donut trick.

Back at his desk, he started working through the list of tasks.

- He needed a website to host the offer, so he modified the same template he'd used before. This took the most amount of time, because he kept updating the template whenever he added or revised something.

- He needed a way for people to contact him. That was simple enough—the template came with a contact form that he connected to his email account.

- He needed a way to get paid. That was easy, too—he just connected his bank account once again and added a button. This time, he even remembered to test the purchase process.

He wrapped up around three a.m. and took a close look at everything. The website was not going to win any design awards. He still had to figure out how to provide the actual service. Time would tell whether it would work or not . . . but Jake was proud.

All things considered, this was an authentic offer, something he felt good about. He was confident that he could help someone who signed up for the service. It also passed the grandparent test—he could easily imagine telling Grandma Norris about it.

When it came time to share the announcement, Jake started to retype what he'd said for his attempt at the negotiation service. But then he had an idea to do something different. He opened up his social feed and composed a detailed message.

He titled the message "My Big Mistake."

Attention, friends and family! I'm starting a new service today, and I wanted to tell you about it—but first, I want to tell you about a big mistake I made. I've been learning a lot about making money apart from my day job. A couple weeks ago, I started buying and selling textbooks and camera gear. In less than a week, I made $1,000!

The guy I've been learning from is kind of a mentor, although he probably wouldn't use that term. He also has a habit of not telling me exactly what to do, so I have to figure it out as I go. Anyway, last week he gave me an assignment to start a new "service business."

Long story short, I thought I had a good idea, but now I know I was totally wrong. I shouldn't have tried to teach people about negotiation. Truth be told, I have a lot to learn about it myself. And besides, my idea wasn't very clearly defined.

Consider it a lesson learned. And here's the good news: *I've got a much better idea.* My new project is called "Student Loan Champion." I want to help people like me who have a lot of debt left over from college.

Come check it out and let me know what you think! And if you know someone who might benefit from it, please pass it on.

He copied the text into an email and sent it to a bunch of his friends, including a link to the new site. After he posted the update and sent the email, Jake sat back in his chair and reflected.

In addition to feeling proud, he was also exhausted. He crawled under his desk and bunched up a couple of spare T-shirts for a pillow. Now that he was sleeping in the back of a car, adjusting to the floor didn't take long at all.

21.

Reputation Associates was hired to conduct an urgent audit of customer opinion regarding Buzzard Co., a social network that recently promised $50 referral fees to users without having enough money to pay them.

To be frank, customer opinion is low, and skepticism is high. The company encouraged users to email everyone in their address books with a single click, yet dramatically underestimated the amount of email that would result from this feature. One user, Bridget Halloway in Lawrence, Kansas, currently has an owed balance of

$76,450 in her referral account. (When reached for an explanation, she informed us that she has a highly engaged book club and a lot of cousins, all of whom she'd signed up for the service.)

In addition, the company's use of consumer data has raised considerable concern. A recent media investigation pointed to the case of a young widow whose husband was killed in an industrial baking accident. The Buzzard system passed sensitive information from his emails to her account just as she was entering a new phase of grief.

We recommend that Buzzard Co. be straight with its users. The company needs to show true contrition without any hint of "passing the buck." An apology without blaming anyone other than the company itself is best. It may also be advisable to remove key management leaders who contributed to this decision.

———

Buzzard Co.
Statement on Recent News Reports
From the desk of the CEO—

We have recently become aware of news reports featuring some unfortunate applications of the Buzzard system. As the Founder, CEO, and COO, I take full responsibility, except in the cases where it's obviously someone else's fault.

Specifically, we regret that the system told Mrs. Alice Mallory in Bloomington, Indiana, that her late husband was not a good match for her, and that he was gay. Our team understands and empathizes with the distress that this has caused.

We're also sorry that the system directed minors to a mature content site that featured a variety of sex acts. While some of these minors may have been pleased to discover this content for the first time, it is definitely not something that should happen again.

These are isolated examples and not reflective of the kinds of decisions that Buzzard recommends to our loyal users every day. We have modified our filters to ensure that adult content will only be shown to adults.

In addition, we have deposited 200 complimentary BuzzBucks™ in Mrs. Mallory's account.

From: Kevin Quan

To: All Staff

Team,

I know it's been a hard couple of weeks, and some of you have questions about our current growth strategy. Rest assured, we have answers! I'm currently seeking a MAJOR round of funding from a top-secret investment group. I can't say more right now, but did I mention it was MAJOR??

In the meantime, the finance dept. would appreciate it if we could all engage in cost cutting wherever possible. We're going to switch Wednesday team lunches from sushi to pizza. And try to go easy on all those Post-its from the office supply room, ha ha.

Sometimes we have to walk through fire to get to the end of the rainbow. In the words of one of my favorite songs, every rose has its thorns . . . but like a unicorn, we shall rise again!!

———

From: Kevin Quan

To: Tom Bosun, Accelerated Investing Group

Tom, just wanted to thank you for agreeing to meet today. I know it will be worth your while!

To recap, Buzzard Co. is seeking an A-round investment of up to $100 million. In just a few short weeks, we've seen our valuation skyrocket to somewhere north of that. We're going places—but we need help!

I trust that your team will be eager to move forward. Let me know if you need info re: wire transfers, share certificates, etc.

———

From: Kevin Quan

To: Inner Circle

Good news!!

We're out of the woods . . . I can't spill the beans just yet, but we're gonna have all the funding we need. I think it's time we planned an all-staff trip to Hawaii. Who's with me??

Aloha nui loa,

K-Quan

———

From: Kevin Quan

To: Tom Bosun, Accelerated Investing Group

Just a heads-up that I'll be out of the office for the next hour. I'll have both cell phones and my tablet with me.

———

From: Kevin Quan

To: Admin

Were there any calls for me?

———

From: Kevin Quan

To: Tom Bosun, Accelerated Investing Group

Just making sure you got my last message? I had my phones but the reception was bad in the massage room, so I might have missed your call.

———

From: Kevin Quan

To: Inner Circle

Bad news. My contact at Accelerated Investing has stopped returning my messages. I'm not sure what happened, but I'm starting to think that we didn't want their money anyway. Those kinds of funding rounds usually come with a lot of restrictions, so we'll be better off elsewhere.

I have a big idea that I want to run by you. Can you come to the break room in fifteen minutes?

———

From: Kevin Quan

To: Our Awesome Users

Fellow Buzzers,

I bring you big news: as Buzzard continues to grow, we're turning down millions in VC money and going directly to you . . . our loyal users!

If you've ever wanted to own a company, or at least a tiny, nonvoting part of a company, now you can.

That's right. We've decided to reject a MAJOR offer of investment capital and pursue crowdfunding instead. In this day and age, no one needs to rely on big-money financiers. We want to invite direct investment from our passionate user base to make sure we can keep buzzing along.

Not only that, but we're offering a series of incentives for our new owner-investors. When you purchase a piece of the future, you can get everything from T-shirts and mugs to the chance to hang out with me for a day. Seriously!

Check out BuzzardCo.com/funding for all the details and special offers.

Living the dream,

Kevin Quan

———

ANDREW MARSHALL SHOW
ONLINE LIVE BROADCAST

Begin transcript at 2:03 p.m., November 20

Andrew: . . . and now let's bring on Kevin Quan, chief exec of that new social network everyone's been talking about. Or should I say *emailing* about? Welcome, Kevin.

Kevin: Thank you, Andrew. And can I say hello to all the Buzzers out there? What's up, party people!

Andrew: Uh, alright. So for our listeners who haven't caught up yet, I wasn't kidding when I said everyone's been emailing about you. But that's not necessarily a good thing, correct? It seems you ran into some trouble.

Kevin: It's true, we had a couple of hiccups. We didn't anticipate how excited everyone would be about our product and referral program. We offered users a very generous bonus—

Andrew: —and you weren't able to pay those bonuses, isn't that right?

Kevin: Technically speaking, our cash reserves underperformed our expectations. We pivoted to making the currency more about sharing the positive message of Buzzard Co. We really appreciate everyone hanging in there with us.

Andrew: It doesn't sound like you're out of the woods yet, but let's move on. Next up are a number of concerns about this "decision-making" model of yours—

Kevin: Can we talk about the new owner-investor program? I thought that's what we were doing here.

Andrew: Yes, but people have a lot of questions about how you're using their data. For example, the system harassed a widow in Indiana with some disturbing news about her late husband.

Kevin: We're really sorry about that. We empathize to her. Or we apologize—whatever. You know what I mean.

Andrew: Shouldn't you be apologizing to her directly?

Kevin: Well, I don't really know her personally. Look, I think what we're doing in terms of allowing people to invest directly is really innov—

Andrew: Thank you, Kevin, that's a great segue. And now we have a surprise for our listeners. My producer Kate is bringing on a special remote guest for the second half of the conversation. Kate, can you and our guest hear me over there?

Kate: Loud and clear. Go ahead, Andrew.

Andrew: Mrs. Mallory, welcome to the program.

Kevin: What?

Andrew: We've arranged for Alice Mallory to join us so you can explain to her exactly how this happened. I'll let you gather your thoughts for a moment.

Listeners, we'll be right back after the break. First, here's a message from our sponsor, Mattress Maven. Are you getting enough sleep? What if you could rest each night on a pillow-filled paradise? Now, thanks to Mattress Maven, you can. If you'd like to get up on the right side of the bed . . .

End transcript at 2:07 p.m.

***

22.

P assengers and crew, welcome to Addis!" Everyone in the cabin around Jake burst into applause as the plane touched down on the runway. *Africa*. More specifically, *Ethiopia*—a new country on a new continent for him.

On the descent, he looked out the window and saw a city teeming with activity. Buildings were being constructed and vehicles were zooming by in every direction—or in some cases, stopped in traffic jams from all directions.

The past couple of days had gone by quickly. After his all-nighter at the office, the next thing he remembered was Clarence shaking him awake in the passenger seat as they arrived at LAX.

Once they were on board, he'd slept for much of the first flight, missing out on an unappetizing lunch that was handed out on plastic trays. He told the woman sitting next to him not to worry about crawling over him if she needed to get up. When he woke up from a deep sleep an hour before landing, he hoped that he hadn't drooled on her.

The second flight, from Munich to Addis Ababa, was different. He sensed an energy shift as soon as he embarked. At least half of the travelers appeared to be Ethiopians either heading home from a trip or flying back to visit relatives. He noticed a jocular air to the conversations and habits. He also observed the unusual carry-on items that many of them were lugging: microwaves, TVs, and coolers that he assumed were full of refrigerated food.

Feeling much more rested, he stayed awake the whole time. He'd lucked out on having a row to himself—Clarence was up front in business class—and he used it as a mobile workstation, alternating between writing in a notebook and typing on his laptop.

Before he left California, he'd figured out the basics of his student loan service. He also had a one-page website that described the service and told people how to sign up.

The response to his social post and email was much better this time. Several people had commented to say they thought it was a great idea. At least two people said they were going to share it with their friends. And even Zach chimed in on the post to say he liked how Jake was sharing the story of his progress, including being honest about the mistake he'd made with the first attempt.

Speaking of Zach, he wondered how he was doing in the new

job. Being so busy with his own problems, he hadn't paid much attention to the news, but he knew that Buzzard was getting a lot of attention—and not all of it was good. Everything about that world seemed so different from what he'd been learning from Clarence. Even though he missed the free meals he'd enjoyed when Zach worked at Titan, he no longer felt jealous of anyone else there. At least for him, the Third Way was the better path.

Thinking of Zach made him think of Maya. After the breakup, he'd backed away a bit to give her the space she'd asked for. He still missed her, though, and a couple times he'd reached out in a low-key, no-pressure way. Right before he left, they had their first phone conversation in what seemed like weeks when he called her from the airport. He wished her a happy Thanksgiving and said that he hoped to meet her family another time, whenever it was right.

He took it as a good sign that she didn't turn him down outright. It was his fault that he'd pushed her away, and he was determined to show her he'd changed.

Then, during the layover in Munich, he'd checked his email and saw another development. Someone had emailed him to ask for help with paying back loans! He and Clarence were close to boarding their flight, so he responded with a quick note saying he'd be in touch within twenty-four hours.

The delay also bought him some time to consider how to respond properly. It was great that he had a potential client, but he needed to think more about how he'd handle the next part of the process.

At Brightside, the company was big on making *workflows*, which were basically diagrams or mind-maps of a process. They could be helpful in getting clients to think more thoroughly about sales and service. Whatever the goal was, you could usually clarify the actions needed by making a workflow.

Jake sketched out a tentative workflow in the notebook:

It looked like a lot, but by building a sequence of events and setting reminders for the check-ins, Jake thought it was manageable. Upon completing the follow-up report, he'd also ask the client for referrals. He made a note to include some sort of referral bonus ("Tell your friends and earn $40 per referral")—but unlike

Buzzard's disastrous program, he'd only pay out when someone became a paying client.

A friendly flight attendant refilled his cup of tea while he was working. He got to talking with her when he went to visit the lavatory and had to wait in the galley for his turn. Her name was Naomi, and she'd only been flying for the airline for a few months. Her goal was to save enough money to go to college and study medicine.

He thought back about how when he went to college, all he had to do was sign a form and tens of thousands of dollars appeared in his account. At the time, his greatest aspiration was to obtain a fake ID and an exemption from the university's foreign language requirement.

Back in his seat, he reviewed the workflow. He now felt more confident about moving forward with the project. He just needed clients, and if all went as he hoped, he'd soon have his first.

When he stepped off the plane, he was in another country—almost. First they had to be bused to the terminal and go through immigration. On the other side of the passport stamp, five days in a place he'd never thought much about until the previous week was waiting for him.

23.

I thought it was just six miles to the city."

Clarence laughed. "Things move a little slower here, Jake. But pay attention, you might learn something."

An hour after arriving at Addis Ababa International Airport, they were in a taxi heading to their guesthouse on the other side of town. On a map, the journey looked short and simple. In the car, it felt like a full-on road trip, complete with some of the most interesting entertainment Jake had ever seen.

The landscape was beautiful, and greener than he'd expected. Everywhere he looked, he saw tall juniper trees with outstretched branches on the side of the highway. And that was just the first half of the journey. The second half took place on a series of bumpy roads, and they were stuck in traffic for longer than they actually moved.

That was when it got interesting. Clarence had said to pay attention, but Jake didn't need to be told. It was impossible to ignore the hubbub of activity that took place right outside his window. Whenever they stopped, a series of roving vendors would approach the vehicle, walking up and down the lanes of stalled traffic.

In one intersection where they were stalled for several stoplight changes, Jake counted more than a dozen people who passed by with goods on display. Some of them offered basic items, including an array of snacks: plantain chips, cans of soda, and something that looked like pretzels.

Others had more elaborate products for sale, ranging from electronics to kids' toys to an entire wardrobe of men's clothes.

Catching Jake's eye, a man approached the window with a giant stuffed panda. The car inched forward before Jake could properly decline this enticing offer.

Another man walked by with a stack of alarm clocks, and something about his appearance registered in Jake's subconscious. "Hey," he said a moment later, "that guy was wearing a Golden State Warriors T-shirt!"

"People love sports here," Clarence responded from the front seat. "Soccer is the most popular, but a lot of basketball players are known worldwide now."

"Yeah, but I'm wondering something. At first I thought, Cool, they like the Warriors here, too—but then I noticed that the shirt said '2019 NBA Champions.' Didn't the Warriors *lose* the championship that year?"

"Ah, I see what you mean," said Clarence. "You're right, and that's probably why that guy is wearing the shirt that celebrates their victory."

Jake looked confused, so Clarence explained further. "When two teams are playing in a major championship series, the franchises know that there will be lots of demand for the winning team's merchandise. But, of course, they don't know who's going to win, and you can't manufacture thousands of shirts and hats instantly—"

"—so they print sets for both teams," Jake interjected.

"Exactly. And places like this are where the ones for the losing team end up. Who knows, maybe you could buy a bunch and resell them back home. It sure would confuse people if you wore one around."

There really is a market for anything.

Clarence turned back around. "So let's consider what you can learn from this. Not just the T-shirt guy, but this whole experience. What do you notice?"

He'd shifted into teacher mode, but Jake didn't mind. His first day in Africa was fascinating, and he hadn't even left the airport taxi yet.

He mentioned what he'd just noticed: that there were all kinds of things that could be bought and sold. It was simply a matter of matching the right buyer with the right seller.

"And the right price," Clarence added. "Don't forget that."

They pulled off the city streets and into a more residential area. There were still plenty of people out and about, but overall it was much quieter than the center of town.

"So think about all those different sellers you saw," Clarence said. "Which one would you want to be?"

"You mean besides the guy with the giant panda? . . . Okay, good question. Well, I probably *wouldn't* want to be one of the people selling sodas and pretzels. It doesn't seem like they could make much money, especially since anyone else could do the same thing."

"Right. Selling a commodity is almost never a good idea. It's a race to the bottom in terms of pricing, and like you said, there's nothing unique about any particular seller."

Jake thought for a moment. "It also seems like it's really important to know your market. One of the guys I saw kept trying to sell me a case of diapers. I suppose he had nothing to lose by trying, but that's not something I plan to need for a long time."

"Yes, that's also a good point," Clarence said. "No matter what part of the world you're in, a lot of people approach selling like a numbers game. In some ways it's true that the more people you ask, the more you'll sell. But for a lot of products, you'll be much more successful by being intentional. It's a lot easier to sell to people who are ready to buy."

Taking notes in the taxi was hard, but Jake managed to scribble down a couple things as Clarence pointed the driver to an upcoming turn, then turned back to look at him again.

"We're almost at the guesthouse, so there's just one more thing I want to mention. The reason why starting your service is so important is because it has the potential to earn money for you even when you're not actively spending time on it. If your entire livelihood depends on you being out on the street all day in the hot sun, what happens if you get sick?"

"You don't get paid that day," Jake said.

"Correct. And the consequences for not getting paid can be dramatic in places like this. For you, the stakes aren't quite as high, but the principle still applies: if you aren't out hustling at flea markets, or otherwise searching for new stuff and then listing it for sale, you won't get paid either. Whereas with the right service, you can work another job, travel, or do whatever else you want while the service is out there marketing itself."

Jake was still in hustle mode. Even though his situation wasn't as extreme as the street vendors, he knew that what he was learning was critical to his future. Somewhere, a money tree was waiting for him. He reminded himself to follow up with Annie, the friend of a friend who'd written to ask about his loan service, as soon as he had Wi-Fi at their guesthouse.

After he carried his bags inside, he came back out to look around some more. He'd been in the country for less than two hours, and it had already made an impact on him. How would he feel after five days?

He had a feeling his life was going to change even more.

24.

When he woke up the next morning, Jake felt confused and refreshed at the same time. The confusion came when he looked outside his window and saw a flock of chickens fluttering about in the front yard. It took him a minute to remember he was more than nine thousand miles from home.

The sense of feeling refreshed came from sleeping in his first real bed in days. Who would have thought he'd have to come all the way to Ethiopia to get a good night's sleep?

Maybe I should look into mattress reselling. All I'd need is a place to store one of them each night.

Entering the dining room, he found a simple breakfast spread laid out with bread, jam, coffee, and fruit. A note from Clarence said that he'd be back at seven thirty to pick him up.

Jake looked at his watch: 7:06. Enough time to grab a shower—not in the gym for once!—and a quick breakfast. They'd be traveling out of the city today, and he was eager to get to know the area more.

As he was finishing up his bread and fruit, he heard a car come to a stop outside. Clarence was in the passenger seat next to a different driver, not the one they'd had from the airport.

"Jake, this is my friend Yonas," said Clarence when Jake hopped in the back.

"Mr. Jake, it is my deepest honor to meet you," said Yonas.

"Nice to meet you, too, Yonas. Just 'Jake' is fine."

"Okay, Mr. Jake. Are you ready to go to the village?"

They set off through the city, where for the first twenty minutes they saw more of the mobile market scene they'd encountered the previous day. Jake was hoping to buy a Warriors shirt for Zach, preferably one with the wrong championship date on it. He was pretty sure he didn't have room for any giant stuffed animals in his carry-on bag.

They didn't stop for either of those items, but when Clarence saw a man lugging a mesh net over his shoulder, he motioned to Yonas to pull over. Yonas waved to the man and they haggled for a few minutes, arguing good-naturedly about a price. When the negotiations had concluded, Clarence reached over from the passenger seat to give the man a few bills in local currency. The man handed over . . . a soccer ball.

"Are we going to play soccer?" Jake asked from the back. Both Clarence and Yonas thought this was funny. Clarence said something about how you never knew when you might need a soccer ball in this part of the world.

Before long, they'd left the main part of the city and the scenery changed. There were still plenty of people milling about at intersections, but everyone seemed much less in a hurry. Yonas pointed out various points of local pride, ranging from mills to markets to a new cell phone tower that everyone was talking about.

Jake thought the last attraction was a little odd—who points out a cell phone tower on a tour of their city?—but when he thought about it more, it made sense. If he didn't have reception in his part of town, and all of a sudden a tower went up that allowed him to communicate, he'd be excited, too.

"By the way," he said from the back, "where *are* we going?"

"Just enjoy the ride and you'll see," said Clarence. Apparently even simple questions resulted in cryptic answers from him.

Jake tried to jot down his observations as they rolled along, but the Land Cruiser kept bumping and jolting every few seconds. He finally gave up and focused on looking out the window. An hour after they'd left the city, Yonas turned down another series of roads, each one less maintained than the last.

At the end of another half hour of turbulent riding, they came to a stop at the entrance to a small village. A crowd was waiting for them. More and more people arrived as they parked the car and got out, including a group of children who seemed very excited to meet Jake. One of the kids kept walking up to him, high-fiving, and then running away in uproarious laughter . . . only to return thirty seconds later for another high five.

While Jake was enjoying his new celebrity status, an older man stepped forward to greet Clarence like a long-lost friend. "Ibrahim, you're looking good!" said Clarence, and the older man laughed as though it was the funniest thing he'd ever heard.

People laugh a lot in this country. Maybe I'll start to get the jokes by day three.

They all followed Ibrahim toward a small hut, where several other people sat waiting for them. "This is the elders of the village, Mr. Jake," Yonas explained. "They will make a welcome for you."

Each of the elders greeted Clarence, and then did the same for Jake, with Yonas making introductions. "You are welcome," several of them said as they took his hand. It took Jake a minute to understand that they meant he was welcome in their home and village.

Someone produced coffee and they sat and drank together. After some discussion of the journey in from Addis Ababa, the first elder who had greeted Clarence stood up and invited everyone else to join him. The whole group left the hut and walked back to the waiting crowd.

They gathered around in a circle and some sort of ceremony began.

One by one, half a dozen villagers stood up to address the group. Each of them began by saying something to the elders, which Jake presumed was a matter of paying respect. This was followed by greeting the guests in a similar manner. Then, each of them told a short story, speaking in their own language while Yonas translated.

The first man looked a bit younger than Clarence. He said his name was Ajani, and he was a baker—a skill he had learned from his father. Ajani was working with his wife and daughters to diversify their family business. They used to bake from home and supply people in the village, but they had recently purchased new equipment and moved headquarters to a larger room in the back of the community center.

The move had allowed them to get a contract with the local school, which was doubly beneficial. In addition to the fact that the school served a lot of lunches, it also ordered the same amount each week.

In the past, Ajani never knew how much bread he'd sell on any given day at the market. With the school contract, he knew that whenever it was open, he could count on a certain amount of money.

Clarence nudged Jake. "Recurring income! This is so important."

Next, a younger man named Kofi stood up. He began with a few words in English before switching to a long string of the local language. As he talked, he held up a display case.

When he finished, he looked at Clarence and Jake. Clarence and Jake looked at Yonas, who had temporarily forgotten his translation duties. Returning to life, he explained that Kofi was a mobile phone reseller.

"These days," Yonas said, "there are more and more phones in the village. Everyone wants one! Many people will save for a long time to buy. But they also need other items—chargers, cases, batteries, and cards that can be topped up for more data and minutes. This guy, he is a one-man phone shop. People in neighboring villages can message him with orders, and once a week he makes rounds. Every other week he goes into Addis and restocks."

When Kofi sat down, Clarence said something to Yonas, who passed the word on to the elders. One of the elders nodded and said something to the group, and then three women stepped forward. Jake made a mental note to ask Clarence about this later.

Lola, Faizah, and Zuri had started a coffee collective. Operating as a partnership, they were able to place bulk orders for green, unroasted beans from local farms. A lot of bigger farms already had suppliers, but they worked with small ones that most distributors ignored.

The mention of coffee made Clarence excited. "My people!" he said. Jake wished he'd thought of that line when the phone reseller was talking.

The stories went on for a while, with the group applauding enthusiastically when each person finished. Finally, the elders looked at Clarence, and he stood to respond. He spoke for a few sentences at a time, allowing Yonas to translate after him.

"Everyone, thank you so much for welcoming us so warmly. It's wonderful to be back, and I'm happy to hear that so many people are starting these projects. I just want to mention two things before we go."

He waited for the translation.

"First, we don't expect every investment to work, so don't be afraid to report about the ones that fail. Sometimes you have to try something for a while to learn that something else might be better."

Another pause.

"Second, you've all been very kind and I appreciate you saying these nice things. However, you are the ones doing all the work. So, congratulations! I hope to hear many good reports in the future."

The small crowd cheered when they heard the translation. Before they could leave, an extensive series of personal greetings was required. Several people pressed small items into Clarence's hands. The mobile phone guy came over to Jake and offered him a free charger.

Right before returning to the Land Cruiser, Clarence remembered something. "Hey, Jake—go grab that soccer ball from the car." He then went back to talk to the elders again.

Before he knew what was happening, Jake was once again surrounded by his fan base of school-age admirers. This time they seemed even more excited. When he handed them the ball, they all lined up for a final high five, then ran off in a pack toward a nearby field. Jake felt like he was a true celebrity, and all he'd done was give them a soccer ball.

That was easy. If I ever want to run for village elder, I know what to do.

——

On the drive back, Clarence explained more about what had happened at the village. "Many of the people there have the same goal as you, Jake. They want to be self-reliant. If they get sick, they want to be able to go to the doctor. They want to have savings. And they know they can't rely on their government or any company to take care of them—so they have to do it themselves."

Jake considered this. "Are you teaching the Third Way model here?"

Clarence shook his head. "This is where it comes from! At least a lot of it. In this part of the world, nearly everyone is an entrepreneur of some kind. They don't have the same kind of job market that we do back home, so they have to get by some other way."

He looked back at Jake while Yonas guided them to the main road. "To answer your question more directly, I'm not teaching much at all. But I thought it would be good for you to see how this works in action. The principles of earning money on your own, whether through buying and selling or offering a service like you're trying to do now, really don't change that much from place to place. What you learn here, you can apply back home."

Back at the guesthouse, they said farewell to Yonas and took a break before dinner. It had been a long day. Even Clarence, who normally operated with the schedule of a twenty-four-hour convenience store owner, looked a little tired.

Jake washed up and connected to the Wi-Fi network. When he checked his email, he had good news waiting for him. Annie had agreed to try the service and had used his online calendar to schedule a call. While he had been bumping along the village roads and enjoying his celebrity status, he'd also received a payment for $150.

A bed to sleep in *and* a $150 payment from a stranger? It was a whole new world.

25.

The time difference between Ethiopia and Oklahoma was nine hours. Not wanting to repeat his time zone mistake, Jake had triple-checked it to be sure. He tested the network and made sure to log on early. Right at the scheduled hour, he pressed a button on his computer and saw a face appear on the screen.

"Annie? Hi, it's Jake."

This was his first client session, or at least something close to it. Annie had said that she had some questions, and he had a few questions for her as well. The Brightside part of him said that he should create an intake interview that clients fill out in advance. That way, he could systemize some of the process and be ready to go as soon as the call started. But he figured that he could always improve along the way. Besides, this was a new experience for him—he wanted to explore and see how it felt.

Annie was twenty-five and had recently returned to her hometown of Tulsa after going to college in Dallas. She earned a degree in elementary education and was now in her second year of teaching fourth grade. Like Jake, she'd taken out a lot of loans to pay for her education. Despite living in the dorms until her senior year and driving an old beat-up Honda to her part-time student job, she had $30,000 to repay.

Jake listened and asked occasional questions. What was her goal?

To not be dealing with this for the next decade, she said. To be able to buy a house and have the mortgage be her only debt.

How did she feel about carrying the loans?

It was a burden, she said. It felt like she'd done something wrong, even though she wanted to be a teacher and didn't have any other way of paying for tuition.

How did she feel right now?

Cautiously hopeful, she told him, but not sure what to do next.

Jake projected confidence, at least much as he could while talking to his first client on a long-distance video link from Ethiopia. He reiterated that he thought he could help her, and if she didn't feel that she had solid practical steps to follow afterward, then he wouldn't keep her money.

Before they hung up, she agreed to make a list of her skills and interests, and he agreed to get to work writing up a plan for her. When he was back from the trip, he'd coach her through the reselling process and include a couple of ideas for doing it in her area. He made a note to focus on opportunities that might be more available in the summer and around holidays, since her time was much more limited the rest of the year. Once she was earning some money, he'd put together a proposed payoff schedule for her loans. He'd been doing the same thing for himself, now that he had at least one new way to get paid.

Evening in North America was early morning in Ethiopia, a day later. When he finished the call, it was time for breakfast. He devoured some local porridge that the guesthouse host prepared and took a second cup of tea back to his room. Yonas was coming in two hours to pick him up, and he wanted to use the time well.

He had a long list of things to do. He wanted to write up his tips for Annie, think through some next steps for marketing, see about listing some more camera gear for selling locally—and those were just the first tasks that came to mind.

Most of all, he wanted to get to work on finding his next clients. In the Third Way forum, there was a whole repository of ideas and resources. That was where he'd learned to make his one-page website. He wanted to go back and look at what else they had that he could use.

Prepared with his list and fortified with tea, he sat down at the laptop. Then everything went off the rails.

He stared blankly at the laptop for several minutes, wondering what to do first. All of a sudden, he felt an irresistible urge to clean up the old icons and documents off his desktop.

Then he started reading a long thread in the forum about social media ads. Jake couldn't spend any money on ads yet, but he read the thread anyway, clicking links that led to other articles, which he left open in new tabs while he went on to something else.

After a while, he opened a new window and logged on to his favorite sports news site. The Warriors were in the midst of a rare losing streak, and he caught up on all the latest injury reports and speculation. The consensus opinion was that either they'd be able to come back soon, or they wouldn't. It took him fifteen minutes of reading to absorb this opinion.

Moving on, he watched and rewatched an amazing video of a cat who'd learned to power on and push a vacuum cleaner around the house. Every time the clip replayed, he thought, *There's no way the cat can do that!* . . . and then it happened again.

He paused for a status check. So far he'd skimmed a dozen articles about something he wasn't ready to do anything about, learned that a professional basketball player might have a problem with his knee, and watched a cat clean an apartment at least five times.

This wasn't going well. Frustrated, he stepped away from his computer.

Yonas was picking him up in ten minutes, and he had to get ready. He'd have to return to this later in the afternoon and try to do a better job.

26.

Yonas was waiting outside in the Land Cruiser. "Mr. Jake! How are you today!"

"I'm good, Yonas, except I can't seem to focus on anything. Where are we headed now . . . Clarence said you had something you wanted to show me?"

"Yes, very much. Come and we will drive there."

They set out for a journey that ended up taking about fifteen minutes. The roving vendors were out and about, and other people were running errands. Yonas pointed to a man with a mattress strapped to the back of a motorcycle. Somehow, he managed to weave through traffic without getting hurt or losing the mattress.

Jake shook his head in wonder. By now he was learning not to be as surprised at such sights.

He was also learning more about the local driving experience, which operated with its own set of rules. When he'd learned to drive back at home, he was taught to use the horn only in case of emergency, like when someone was crossing into your lane and didn't see you.

Here, the opposite was true: the frequent use of the horn seemed to be mandatory. Yonas honked when he was changing lanes, when the traffic light changed colors, and whenever traffic was stopped for more than a few seconds. He waved to a guy he knew and honked. He shook his fist and honked at a truck that cut them off. When they finally pulled up to a building and parked, he turned off the engine and honked to announce his arrival.

Idea for my next visit here: buy a bunch of earplugs, walk up and down the street offering them to pedestrians. Possible name: Earplug Champion.

They walked into a small storefront that had been set up as a makeshift factory. A woman who looked to be about twenty years old approached and Yonas introduced them.

"This is my daughter, Eshe." He pronounced it with two syllables: *Esh-ee.*

"Hi, Eshe. Nice to meet you . . . I'm Jake."

"Look," said Yonas, "she is making bags for sale to visitors!"

Eshe was a little embarrassed. "They aren't ready yet, Father! But here you can see a prototype."

Jake was looking at three large tables, each laid out with fabric, stretched leather, and several types of buttons and zippers. On the last table, a handbag appeared to be fully assembled. When he picked it up, it felt well made and built to last.

"This is really cool," he said. "Is it going to be your business?"

"I hope so!" she said. "It is a—what do you call it?—an experiment."

Eshe showed him around, pointing out different materials and tools. He was impressed with how orderly everything was, with each item in its place and a clear process for assembling the bags.

"How did this start?" he asked.

She explained that through her dad's tour guide business, she'd noticed that most visitors carried bags of some kind wherever they went. Backpacks, messenger bags, laptop bags, purses of various types—almost everyone had at least one, and many people had several that they used for different purposes.

But even though there was no shortage of bags, most of them fit into one of two categories. Most of the backpacks were cheap and poorly made. There wasn't anything distinctive about them, and they often fell apart after a few trips to the village.

Other bags were better made, but they came with a much higher price tag. When Eshe asked one of her father's clients how much it had cost, she was astounded at the answer. It was several months' wages for the average person in her country.

It also gave her an idea.

She had grown up sewing and liked to work with her hands.

Her uncle, Yonas's brother, was a tailor—so she had access to equipment and knowledge. One thing led to another, and she ran with the vision. She spent Sundays strolling through markets and looking at all the different bags for sale. Most of them looked alike, she noticed, and a large number of them were mass-produced in Asian factories.

Many of Yonas's clients, and a lot of foreign visitors in general, seemed to be searching for the "real" Ethiopia when they came to the country. If she could make a better bag, playing up the hand-made connection, she could sell it for less than the luxury bags with the shocking price tag, but still far more than it would cost in materials and labor. And if there was enough demand, she could hire local women to make the bags, allowing her to focus on running the business.

At some point the vision expanded, because she realized that even if she made and sold bags to every one of Yonas's visitors, it would still be a small market. What she needed was a way to reach people overseas who couldn't visit, but still liked the idea of buying something authentic that came from this part of the world—especially if the product was well made and employed local workers.

That was where Clarence came in. On his last trip here, when he'd met with the village elders to understand how he could be helpful, he'd also met with Eshe and given her some advice. On this trip, they were going to meet again to talk more specifically about starting a crowdfunding campaign to raise awareness from potential supporters around the world.

Jake had to get back—he really needed to work on that report—but seeing Eshe in action was inspiring. He was already thinking about the campaign and wondering if he could help somehow. He could make a pledge, of course, but maybe he could also help to share her story.

She wasn't looking for a handout. She wanted to grow her business.

And if it didn't work out, he was going to recommend she consider selling earplugs.

27.

Back at the guesthouse, Jake sat down at his laptop again. Then he stood back up. Something about that morning's work session had led to him getting distracted. That was how he'd ended up spending his time on basketball injuries and cat videos. He needed to do something differently.

He thought back to that time when he'd written his term paper the same morning it was due. The urgent deadline would have caused any other student to panic. But Jake didn't panic—he got to work. That deadline had actually worked in his favor, inspiring him to push through and complete the assignment just in time.

Now, he tried to re-create a similar mindset. He started by closing down every tab on his computer that didn't directly relate to one of the items on his task list. Then he got serious, scanning the list to identify the three most important tasks:

1. Follow up on the auctions that had closed since leaving home
2. Complete a draft of the report for Annie
3. Attempt to find the next client for Student Loan Champion

He promised himself he wouldn't do anything else until he'd made real progress on each of these things.

The first task was so simple that he wasn't sure why he hadn't knocked it out earlier. He had to invoice three buyers, respond to a couple of questions, and list another economics book from the bulk set he'd purchased. Preena had generously offered to pick up the shipments that arrived at his old apartment, as well as mail out any orders that couldn't wait until his return. He sent her a quick note to update her on the details.

It didn't take long, and when he finished he felt a small sense of accomplishment. Every listing improved his cash flow situation, and every sale got him closer to the goal of getting back on his feet and paying off those loans. But he resisted the urge to celebrate. Instead, he stood up again, stretched, and walked around the room briefly. Then he sat back down and set a timer on his phone for thirty minutes. During that time, he'd do nothing except work on his report for Annie.

When the timer went off, he wasn't finished, but he'd made good progress. Another couple of sessions like that and he'd have a solid report. Also, since he assumed that Annie's problems and potential solutions weren't entirely unique—lots of teachers had student loan debt they wanted to pay off—he figured that whatever he did now could save him time later.

His third task was to work on finding his next client. He didn't want to be a one-hit student loan wonder.

He thought back on the Third Way model. Since most people who used it had day jobs and other commitments, the model recommended that you do at least three small things every day to market your business. The three things didn't need to be big projects—even just sending an email asking for a connection would count. The key was to make sure you were choosing the right things, and then to do them consistently.

Jake thought about how he'd arrived at his current status. Annie was a friend of a friend who'd mentioned Student Loan Champion to her. Assuming the session worked out, he could ask her for a referral when they finished, but not yet. Where were all the *other* Annies? That was what he had to figure out.

Instead of researching ads that he wasn't prepared to pay for, he decided to learn more about his ideal customer. He tried to put himself in that person's shoes. If he was a couple years younger and dealing with this problem, what would he do? The answer was obvious: he'd go online and search "pay off my student loans" or something similar.

He typed in the phrase now. Thanks to the wonders of modern technology, in less than a second he had a dozen results on his screen, several of which appeared to be good leads. Hopping onto a forum, he scanned through a number of discussion threads. This could be worth looking at closer and maybe even participating in, he thought. He made a note to research it further during his next session.

Next, he sent an email to his college alumni office, letting them know about the project. He wasn't sure if anything would come of it, but he figured he might as well try. If he could get a contact there, perhaps they could mention him to some of the students who came into the office feeling worried about their loans.

Working through his list and fighting off the desire to procrastinate felt good. He sat back and began to reflect on the day.

Everything else disappeared from his mind when he refreshed his inbox and saw a new message.

This time it wasn't a loan collection notice. The Mazda hadn't flooded, leaving him confined to a mobile water park for a bedroom. And whatever problems he had with the assessment at his day job, he'd have to deal with later.

The new message was an email from Maya.

Stop the presses. This was even better than a cat on a vacuum cleaner.

28.

On the surface, there was little that was notable about Maya's email.

Jake, of course, spent forty-five minutes deconstructing the message for every possible subtext.

From: Maya Alvarez
To: Jake Aarons
Hey there. I was thinking about you and wanted to say hi. The other day I went on a hike with Jamie and it reminded me of our first hike.

Things have been busy here. The annual report is due right after Thanksgiving, and we've had some new clients move

into our system. But I'm holding things together and I still
really love the work.

　　How is your trip going? I hope you're having a good time
and learning a lot. From what you've told me about him,
Clarence seems really interesting.

　　Well, I guess I should wrap this up and get back to that
report. Whatever happens with us next, I wanted you to
know that you've been on my mind. Give me a call when you
get home and we can catch up more.

　　Take care,

　　Maya

He didn't have a conference room with a whiteboard and dry-erase markers in the guesthouse, but he imagined being at the office with his fellow consultants, breaking down each sentence to discern its full meaning.

"I was thinking about you and wanted to say hi . . ."

That seemed like a good start.

"Whatever happens with us next . . ."

Ruh-roh. That sounded like something you'd say to your friend at summer camp before never seeing them again. He assigned it a lower score on the imaginary whiteboard assessment tool.

"Give me a call when you get home . . ."

Okay, great! All was right with the world. He'd call the moment the plane touched down at LAX.

Jake spent another half hour considering his response. Finally, after a lot of backing up and starting over, he looked at what he had written.

From: Jake Aarons

To: Maya Alvarez

Hey, Maya!

It's really great to hear from you. I'm glad you're staying busy. Not surprised that you can handle the whole office by yourself! No one could accuse you of not being a hard worker. :)

Yeah, Clarence is awesome. I'm learning a lot here, and I want to tell you all about it. But first, I want to be totally honest with you about some stuff. As you know, I've been having a hard time lately, and I haven't really told you the whole story. Remember when I said I had "some debt" from Cal State? To be totally truthful, it's more like $50,000 of debt. I felt ashamed about it, especially knowing how hard your family has worked since your grandparents first came to the States. Also, here I am in this country where a soccer ball is a luxury . . . it all brings some perspective into your life, or at least it does for me.

The good news is, I'm working on it! With what I'm learning, I'll be able to make a solid plan to pay off those loans. It seriously feels like my whole life is changing, and for the better.

One more thing. Remember when I canceled our dinner plans at the last minute? I wasn't just being a jerk, or at least not on purpose. I got a call at work that my apartment was flooded. When I showed up, everything was a huge mess. Of course, I forgot to pay for renter's insurance back when I signed the lease, so I had to pack up as much stuff as possible and get creative.

I felt embarrassed and mad at myself, and I just thought it would be better not to bother you about it. I'm really sorry

that it felt like I was ignoring you. I hope that we can regroup
in lots of ways, but I want to be a better friend to you no
matter what we do.

   And yes! I'll give you a call as soon as I'm back. Enjoy your
family visit and eat a tamale for me . . .

He then spent another fifteen minutes trying to decide how to
end the message. There were a surprisingly large number of search
engine results for "how to sign off an email." *Your friend* didn't feel
quite right. *Love* seemed a little awkward, at least at the moment.

   *New business idea: a ghostwriting service, specializing in emails to
the girlfriend who recently left you.*

   He finally ended with "Thinking of you."

   Then he looked it over again—in other words, he reread it six
times—and hit send. All things considered, the day had turned
out fairly well.

29.

Back in California, the Third Way group was settling in for their next meeting. Jake and Clarence were joining in remotely, just before sunrise in Addis. When they logged on to the video link, the first thing they saw was Adrian stirring a can of something that looked suspiciously like instant coffee.

"Hey, Clarence! This stuff is really good," he said with a smile.

"It really is," agreed Celia, leaning over to wave hello through the screen. "You should try it. It's almost better than the Honduras blend from last week, especially when you add a lot of milk and sugar."

Clarence wasn't buying it. "Nice try, you guys. I know you miss me."

After a bit of laughter and chitchat from the group, he leaned back in to say that he was going to take a break. "Folks, I had six meetings with new business owners yesterday, so I'm going to go back to bed for a bit. Don't burn down the place without me! I look forward to seeing you next week."

The group said farewell, and Adrian asked for volunteers to share updates.

"I'll go," said a woman Jake hadn't seen before. "Hi, Jake. I'm Keisha. I don't think we've met yet."

Jake waved hello from a video screen nine thousand miles away.

"I'm a travel nurse, so I'm often away on assignment," Keisha said. "That's also what my project is about. There are a lot of other travel nurses out there, and a bunch of websites where we all gossip about assignments. But the process of becoming a travel nurse can be intimidating. Some agencies are better than others, and some should really be avoided altogether.

"It really is a fantastic opportunity for the right person. My last assignment was in Miami, which was fun. Before that I had six weeks in Aspen. They aren't all luxury assignments, but going to any new city to work for a while can be a good experience. Plus, all your bills are paid, including the flights to your assignment city and a furnished apartment.

"So anyway," she continued, "I'm creating a guide to help other people who want to do this. I bet I can save them a lot of time and hassle . . ."

"And that's worth something!" Jo broke in, waving hello to Jake before continuing. "This is a really great idea."

"You think so?" asked Keisha. "I wasn't sure, but when I emailed Clarence about it last week, he also seemed enthusiastic."

"Definitely," said Adrian. "It has all the characteristics of a strong offer. Just think about it. First, you have a really clear target market."

"People who want to become travel nurses," said Keisha.

"Well, not quite," said Adrian. "It's more like *people who are already nurses* who want to learn how to get the best travel assignments, right? You're not providing nursing training."

He went on to explain more, taking on the role that Clarence usually filled. "The difference matters because the language you use will be different. For this project, I think you want to talk directly to nurses. No one else."

Listening to the conversation, Jake was learning from afar. He made a note and underlined what he'd just realized: he had to speak to people who had the problem he was targeting—no one else.

Adrian kept going. "Then, you've got a clear *problem*. If a nurse is interested in a travel opportunity, how do they learn about it? Right now, that nurse's friend tells them about it. Or they search online and wade through a ton of info, some of which is biased or misleading. In other words, it's all a bit random."

Celia jumped in to continue. "So your *solution* is that you'll clear all of that up. You're an unbiased source—you don't represent an agency or hospital, and you've had a lot of personal experience. You can show nurses what they need to know to get the best assignments, and make sure they avoid common mistakes."

Adrian returned to finish the thought. "To bring it full circle, it's like Jo said. This is valuable!" Everyone nodded in agreement.

The group continued to talk about Keisha's travel nurse guide, batting around ideas and questions. The primary benefit of the guide was providing clarity. It had the potential to save aspiring travel nurses a lot of time and wasted effort. Therefore, Preena said, it was important that she communicate this benefit from the very beginning.

Keisha also wasn't sure what format was best—should it be a simple report, an interactive online course, or something else? The group had a heated debate about the pros and cons to each, with Adrian firmly believing that a course was best, and Celia siding with a couple others in keeping it simple with just a report. Keisha said she saw the appeal of each option, so she'd email Clarence again and ask him to weigh in as a tiebreaker.

When they wrapped up the discussion, she was excited. "Thanks, you guys!" she said. "I'll try to have something further for you next week."

"Awesome," said Adrian. "Who's next?"

Jake spoke up from afar. "Can you all hear me okay?" Seeing a few thumbs-up signs, he continued.

"Great to see you all! I don't want to monopolize the meeting, especially since I'm all the way over here and you were all so help-ful last time. I'd just like to give you a quick update on a big change I made since we last talked."

He ran through his update on how he'd decided to abandon his first idea and try another. The update ended with him telling the story of his repositioned service and first client.

"This is amazing!" Keisha said. "I'm glad you were able to re-group."

"Me, too," he said. "But I'm not sure I would have understood the problem with the first idea if it wasn't for this group. This second idea feels much stronger."

Over the next hour, the group ran through more updates. They spent some time helping Marta get her test-prep site to rank higher in search results. Then, Jo shared a tool she'd been using to help automate some of her most common tasks.

Before the meeting wrapped up, Jake had one final question for everyone. "By the way, I've been wondering something. How did this all start?"

Adrian took the question literally. "Tonight? Well, you called in from your computer and we saw your face on the screen here at the coworking space. Technology is pretty amaz—"

"No, no . . ." Jake laughed, with a bit of a delay from the video transmission. "That's not what I meant."

"You mean the Third Way group?" It was Celia's turn now.

"Yeah!" said Jake. "I finally understand what it's about, but I don't know how it began."

"You haven't heard that story?" Celia asked. "You should definitely ask Clarence about it. It's a big part of why we're all here."

The group was starting to pack up. Jake thanked them again and said he'd see them in person for the next meeting.

When he disconnected from the video call, he thought about what Celia had just said. Not only did he not know how the group started, he was also in the dark about something else.

He didn't know much at all about the person he'd just accompanied halfway around the world.

30.

What he knew was that Clarence had been in the navy. For how long, he wasn't sure, but he sensed that it was an important milestone in his life. A lot of Clarence's mindset of order and self-discipline seemed to have come from those years.

He knew that he'd been married before, maybe when he was in the service or shortly thereafter. Jake didn't *think* he had any kids, but he wasn't positive.

He knew that he'd gone on to start a series of businesses, one of which was a big failure. Preena had told Jake something about how that experience had led Clarence to rethink how he approached his projects, which eventually morphed into the model he called the Third Way.

Since then he'd started and advised on a number of projects, never again trying to scale a business like he'd done when he was younger, but eventually settling into his role as mentor and philanthropist.

Jake knew, of course, about Clarence love of coffee, the fact that he'd been to Ethiopia several times, and many other places around the world as well.

This left a lot of gaps to fill in.

Clarence Johnson, who emphasized the importance of storytelling in the projects he advised on, didn't talk much about his own story. He was uncannily good at getting other people to talk about themselves. He deflected praise and genuinely seemed to enjoy advising his students on their projects.

This was all admirable, of course. And his wisdom seemed to come from experience. Jake thought back to a conversation they'd had after visiting the village.

That day had been a lot to take in, but the main point seemed to be centered around something Clarence told him on the ride home. All over the world, people longed to make a living and provide for their families. The basics of starting a real business without spending a lot of money weren't that different. Access to networks and a financial safety net were what separated this part of the world from their own.

"We need to look out for ourselves and each other," Clarence said. "And don't forget, Jake, you can do more than you think."

At the end of the day they'd ended up on the porch of their

guesthouse, drinking iced hibiscus tea that the innkeeper had prepared. Even Clarence had a limit on the amount of caffeine he could consume each day.

"There were two more things from today that I wanted to ask you about," Jake said.

"Go for it."

"First, after the two guys in the village—the baker and the phone reseller—stood up to tell their stories, you said something to Yonas, who said something to the elders. What was that about?"

Clarence thought for a moment. "Oh, right. I was a little worried that all the men were going to dominate the presentation. I knew that those ladies had formed the coffee collective, so I tried to politely make the hint that we wanted to hear from both men and women.

"It can be a tricky thing," he continued, "because I'm not here to dictate how village life in Ethiopia should be run. After all, we have plenty of problems and issues in our country, too. That said, I've noticed that all over the world, a lot of women tend to be even more resourceful and hardworking than the guys. So I like to give a gentle nudge toward making sure they have a chance to be heard."

"Gotcha," said Jake. "The second thing was when we were heading back to the car, and—"

"The soccer ball," said Clarence.

"Yeah!" He'd read his mind.

"Right, so I knew the soccer ball would be a big hit. It cost less than $10 and will provide endless entertainment to dozens of kids. But I also don't want to just walk around handing stuff out. It's disrespectful, and it can reinforce the mindset that somehow we're superior to them just because we have money to spend on games and they don't.

"In this case," he continued, "I had a relationship with them and I've been to the village twice before—so I thought it was okay. But just to make sure, I went to talk to the elders so they knew what was happening."

"Wow, that makes sense," said Jake. "I never would have thought about it that way."

"Most people don't. But just like anything else in life, we can only be responsible for what the universe places in our path. Somehow I started coming here five years ago, so this is what I can do. A lot of folks here are far more resourceful than all of us back home. I just try to help out where I can without trying to take over or impose my own way of doing things."

Clarence is a smart guy, Jake thought. The more he learned, the more impressed he was.

But, he realized after thinking about it some more, he still wondered about how he got started with the Third Way in the first place.

Later that day, after Clarence had taken a nap and Jake had done more work on his auctions—he needed Preena's help to ship out a few items, and he had a new idea of selling some digital products to complement his textbooks and camera gear—they sat down again.

"Hey," Jake said. "You never really told me much about how you got into all of this. I've been wondering!"

"Oh," said Clarence. "Well, it's always hard to know where to begin that story. Have you ever heard of the Falkland Islands?"

"Maybe," said Jake. "They're near . . . South America?"

"Exactly, off the coast of Argentina. When I was in the navy, we ended up docking there in the midst of a fourteen-day sail with no other stops. Back then, there wasn't much of an internet, and you had to use prepaid phone cards to call home whenever the ship was docked in port."

Most sailors picked up a couple of phone cards before departure, Clarence explained, but he did some research and learned an interesting fact: the Falklands were a disputed territory, geographically close to South America but claimed by Britain. Argentina also claimed rights to the territory, and there had even been a war between the two countries a few years earlier. Britain emerged as the victor, and most residents of the Falklands spoke English. But as a consequence of being located much closer to South America, there were a few quirks that made the islands unique.

One of those quirks was that all telecommunications were routed through Argentina, and most prepaid phone cards from the United States didn't work—except for the brand that Clarence had gone out of his way to purchase.

"Interesting," Jake said as Clarence came to this point of the story. "So you were a phone card reseller?"

"That's right. Kind of like those guys you see on the streets here!

Except I was on a ship with a deck full of sailors who had all promised to call home, and I had the unique advantage of owning the
only phone cards that worked."

He sold them at a surcharge, tripling his investment, and no one
complained. If it wasn't for his stash, they'd have no option at all.

"That's awesome!" Jake said. "And from there, you just . . .
moved on to the Third Way?"

"Not quite." Clarence chuckled. "I did a few other small things
like the phone card hustle after I got out of the service, and most
of them worked fairly well. So after a while, I thought I could do
no wrong. Big mistake!"

He checked his phone. "But it's almost time for dinner, so let's
save the rest of the story for another time."

Jake and Clarence were meeting Yonas, Eshe, and a few others
that evening. Sure enough, right after he returned to the living
room from changing his shirt, he heard the telltale honk of the
Land Cruiser.

"Mr. Clarence! Mr. Jake!" Yonas yelled out the window, adding
another honk for enthusiasm. "I hope you are hungry!"

31.

The Olympic time trials were starting soon, and Jake was in the lead. He just had to maintain his pace to the finish line, which was, what, only another twenty-three miles? He imagined the medal, the podium, the national anthem. Crowds of people cheered as he ran past and waved, occasionally returning their greetings in the local language.

When he returned to reality, there was no time trial, no cheering crowds, and he was only running three or four miles in total. But he was having fun. Upon arrival in Addis, Jake had felt a little queasy. Most Western visitors needed time to adjust to the altitude, more than seven thousand feet above sea level. By his last day, he was feeling better and excited to see the city on foot.

Lacing up his shoes and heading out, he jogged toward Meskel Square, a central gathering point that served as a free outdoor gym. Along the crescent-shaped track, dozens of people ran back and forth, especially at the peak times of sunrise and sunset. Huge billboards for banks, beer, and politicians beamed out over the crowd.

Crossing the traffic to get to the square was the hardest part. He made his way past a dozen streets and small intersections, giving a thumbs-up to a roving vendor whose miscellaneous wares consisted entirely of goods stamped with the image of Leonardo DiCaprio.

After half a mile he felt like a native—at least until he came to a massive traffic circle, where he stopped in his tracks as vehicles zoomed past him in every direction. There was no traffic light and no crosswalk. How in the world was he supposed to get across?

He found his answer as he watched a group of women carrying baskets on their heads. A few of them had babies wrapped tightly in brightly colored cloth that hugged their bodies, while others were pushing carts of items to sell at the market. No one traveled light here, it seemed. They appeared to be crossing directly in the middle of traffic, yet the motocross racers and minivans that served as communal taxis magically veered to one side or another as they approached.

Jake still wasn't sure how it worked, but he jumped in behind the women and managed to cross to the other side. Somehow, it seemed, there was order in the chaos.

It was much easier after that. He relaxed in the pedestrian-only area and ran his three miles before heading back to the guest-house.

With each lap he kept thinking about the eventful month he'd been having. A few weeks ago, he wasn't sure he could pinpoint Ethiopia on a map. Now, after just a few days here, it felt like a place he would remember forever.

And it wasn't just about the specific place. He was changing, too. Until he'd taken on the first assignment, he hadn't ever really earned money on his own, at least not consistently. He certainly hadn't ever set up a website, offered himself for hire, and signed a client in forty-eight hours. He also hadn't faced as much uncertainty as he'd encountered recently: getting kicked out of his apartment, realizing how much debt he was in, struggling at work, and losing Maya.

No, he'd just been floating along, and not in a good way. Even just a few years ago, he'd had *goals*. What were they? He tried to remember as he ran along. An image of climbing Kilimanjaro popped into his head. Wasn't that somewhere near here? He made a mental note to do some research later. Maybe he and Zach could take the trip together.

He remembered the idea to pay for Liza's hostel stays when she went on her gap-year trip to Asia. Crazy as it was, considering his current financial status, he really hoped he could make it happen. He was proud of her, and he wanted to do whatever he could to support her dreams.

He had some dreams of his own, too, including some that were just beginning to form. What he was learning wasn't just an answer to his immediate problems, it felt like a beginning to a whole new life. He wasn't sure how he'd arrived at this juncture of crisis and opportunity, but he was looking forward to discovering where it would take him. It was clear that financial independence was key to many parts of whatever came next, and now he felt it might actually be in reach.

Jogging back to the guesthouse, he made a mental note of something else he had to do. The next day, before they left, he spent an hour writing postcards while sitting at a café. He sent one to Maya, of course, and others to Zach, Liza, and their parents.

He saved his last postcard for Preena, thanking her again for the incredibly generous gift of a plane ticket. "I wouldn't be here if it wasn't for you," he said. "And I'm so glad you invited me to the group."

32.

The in-flight entertainment system seemed to be broken, or maybe it was just a reflection of what most Hollywood movies were like these days. It promised something like forty movies on demand. Instead, the same superhero movie played over and over on a loop.

Maybe they meant you could see one movie forty times before the flight was over.

Jake was restless. Flying to a new place was always exciting, but going home felt like backtracking. He'd lucked out on the way over with a whole row to himself, but this time he was trapped in the middle seat with no room to spare. The hours wore on, and the superhero on the screen was nearly defeated before miraculously recovering to save the world. And then, in a stunning development, he did it all over again.

They landed in the late afternoon, and Clarence dropped him off at the office two hours later. As he unloaded the bags, he thanked his host one more time.

"Clarence, I'll try to find a better way to tell you later, but for now—thanks so much. This was an incredible experience for me."

"Oh, I was glad to have you there," Clarence said. "You're on to something, Jake. And don't forget, you can do more than you think."

He drove off and Jake walked into the office, wondering what would be waiting for him.

When he opened the door, he wasn't prepared for what he saw. Chaos. Destruction. Chairs were overturned and the place had been ransacked. FBI agents stood guarding the computers while Sloan was in handcuffs, asking for a lawyer.

At least that was how he'd imagined it. In reality, the office was just the same as it was before he'd left. He opened the door, a couple of people waved, and he went to his desk.

What was really waiting for him was a note from Jan for him to get started on a new account.

Brightside had recently signed a new client, an independent music label that was struggling to adapt to industry changes. It was a small contract, but the word was that Magnate was particularly interested in it. Apparently the label's CEO had started it on a whim and was largely absent from day-to-day management—but he had close relationships with several people at much larger firms. Magnate hoped to use the relationship to gain the business of the big companies.

Jan said that she wanted him to jump in right away. "If we get this right, it could help the whole office," she told him.

"I'm ready," he said. And he *felt* ready. Despite just getting off two long flights, first to Germany and then home, he was eager to work.

Right before returning, he'd also lined up plans to tour three new apartments in the next few days. If all went as he'd hoped, he'd move into one of them before another week went by.

For now, though, it was still home sweet Mazda. At the end of the day he returned to the car, which he'd left in Brightside's lot while he was away. He stretched his legs, drove to his designated parking spot near the gym, and was asleep within two minutes of crawling into the backseat.

He was wide awake a few hours later.

A quick glance at his phone confirmed it was now afternoon in Ethiopia. The time zone difference was no joke. His mind was confused . . . but his body felt strangely well rested. It was as though he'd consumed a large energy drink while he'd been dozing for the past couple of hours. After fifteen more minutes had passed with no change in status, he gave up and drove back to the office. He had an idea about how to help the record label.

Starting work at three a.m. was different from working *until* three a.m. As long as you didn't think too much about the inevitable upcoming crash, you actually gained energy as you went along instead of losing it.

Outlining his idea, Jake typed like a madman—maybe he really *had* consumed an energy drink in his sleep—and before long he looked up and saw that he had four full pages of notes.

Sometime later he glanced out the window and saw the sun coming up. He was starving. Checking his phone for the nearest diner, he found one that looked good—or at least it looked *open.* He drove there and ate breakfast while reviewing the draft of what he'd written.

Yeah, this is definitely an unconventional approach. It's the kind of thing that could either get you promoted or fired.

When he finished his pancakes, he sent a message to the team asking if they could meet when everyone got in. Two hours later they were all assembled in the conference room.

"Okay, Jake," Jan said. "What's this top-secret plan of yours?"

"It's a plan for Rattlesnake Records," he said. "And the secret is hiding right in front of them. They're trying to revive a business model that doesn't work anymore. Instead of fighting for it, they should give it up and move on."

"Interesting," Jan said. "Keep going."

"Right now they're way too spread out. Even though 40 percent of their revenue comes from traditional album sales, the amount of that revenue continues to decline every quarter. I mean, think about it—do any of you buy albums anymore, or even single songs? The future is all streaming, all the time.

"So that's why they need to let it go," he continued. "The money they're making now isn't worth what it's costing them to deny the facts. Next, they need to learn something that I observed in Ethio—"

Sloan interrupted him. "Hold on, let me get this straight. You would tell the client to give up a revenue source that's been coming in every month for years?" He looked around the room, assuming that everyone else was just as skeptical.

"I think we should listen to Jake," said Preena.

Thanks, Preena.

"Absolutely," said Jake. "They shouldn't just transition or 'pivot,' they should completely drop the old approach. But as I was saying, there's more to it. Let me tell you a quick story."

He turned to face Jan and Preena, blocking Sloan's line of sight and preparing to ignore any further interruptions.

"Last week I met this guy, Yonas, who's trying to build a little business as a tour guide for foreigners visiting Ethiopia. There are a lot of foreigners coming to town each week, but when he first tried to recruit them as clients, he wasn't that successful. It was only after he changed tactics and began *ignoring* a lot of what other tour guides were doing that he ended up coming out ahead of everyone else.

"So this music label, Rattlesnake Records, the more they try to split the difference, the more they're going to struggle. They need to go all in on one thing, one approach, and one fan base."

"And one band, too? That seems really risky," said Preena.

"Not one band or one artist," he clarified. "But one *type* of band or artist. There should be a very clear unifying theme among everyone they sign. It doesn't even need to be the same type of music. It's more about the same values. I wrote more about that on page two of the draft report I just sent you. There are some examples and projections on the next few pages."

He finished and sat down. He half expected the room to erupt in applause, which didn't happen. He really should work on his endings.

"It's still risky," Jan finally said. "But it's also interesting.

"Let's prepare two plans," she decided. "We'll present Jake's first and tell them it's a bit out of the ordinary. Then, if they don't like it, we'll be ready with some more typical recommendations."

The meeting broke up as everyone went back to work. Aside from the imaginary applause, Jake figured that presenting his plan as an option to the client was as good of an outcome as he could have hoped for.

It was nine a.m. and suddenly he was hungry for lunch.

33.

The most memorable events in Jake's life had included some fairly normal rites of passage, such as graduating from high school and the European trip he'd taken with Zach. He also remembered scoring the game-winning goal in his fifth-grade soccer tournament. Then, of course, there was the day he beat Metal Gear Solid 3 on expert mode, a feat that he proudly listed on his college applications.

Before most of those days, he'd felt a surge of nervous anticipation. How would it feel when he walked across that stage to receive the diploma? After trying and failing over and over to beat the end boss in Metal Gear, would today really be the day?

This felt like another one of those critical times. Following days of silence and a slowly rekindled friendship by email while he was away, he was going to see Maya for the first time since the train wreck of an anniversary dinner. He'd called her after landing at the airport, and they'd arranged to meet for coffee two days later. Fittingly, he invited her to the Lava Java.

She pulled up in her Subaru and met him inside, where he'd been waiting with a table. It wasn't a fancy restaurant, but he'd arrived twenty minutes early on principle. And while he was pretty sure he had more than $4 in his checking account, when he bought her coffee, he paid with cash just to be safe.

"It's good to see you, Jake." She sat down.

He thought that meant it was good to see him.

"I've been looking forward to it!" he said. "I even washed my home for you." When Maya looked confused, he pointed sheepishly to the Mazda.

"Jake! I can't believe you've been sleeping in your car all this time. Why didn't you tell me sooner?"

Well, for a while you didn't want to talk to me. And before then, I was afraid to out myself as a loser.

"It just didn't feel right. But I'm glad I came clean with you when I was away. And anyway, I think I've found a new place. I'm going to see it right after our meeting. If it works out, maybe you can come by this weekend?"

She sat in silence for a few moments while Jake tried to act casual. He decided to move on without waiting for a response.

"Oh! Before I forget, I got you something from Ethiopia."

He handed her a wrapped present. She opened it and looked up.

"It's . . . a journal? This looks really nice."

"Yeah, I was thinking about something you said one day. You mentioned how so much of your work is for other people, and you wished you had some time for yourself. With the new year coming up, I thought you could use this to write down some of your goals. And, you know, follow along with them . . . maybe write down what happens."

He'd practiced everything except the last part.

"Thanks so much. This is really sweet of you."

"You're welcome," he said as he relaxed. "I almost got you a T-shirt with the wrong NBA championship team on it, but I figured this was better."

There had been a long line of coffee orders in the queue. After a few more minutes, the barista called out their names and Jake went to collect the cups. It was funny—Maya seemed more nervous about their meeting than he did. What did that signify? It was as though the dynamic in their relationship had shifted ever so slightly. No doubt he would spend several hours processing it after she left. For now, he wanted to tell her about his new business.

Returning with his double espresso and Maya's almond milk latte, he began to explain everything that had happened in the past couple of weeks. He told her about how he'd made $1,000 in just a few days, thanks to his assignment from Clarence. He told her about the first attempt at his service business, and then his second. He ran through Sloan's antics at the office, the flooded apartment, and his day in the village where he became a celebrity for handing over a soccer ball.

She seemed impressed. "All of this happened since we last met? I thought *I* had been busy! It's really great that you're learning so much."

"I *am* learning," he said. "But like I said in that first email, I'm sorry I wasn't more open with you about what was going on."

Maya sat there for a minute, as if considering how to respond.

"Let's hold off on that conversation for now," she finally said. "But listen, the student loan service you're trying made me think of something. You know that when I did AmeriCorps, they paid off most of my loans, right? It's part of the incentive package they use to recruit volunteers. You don't make much money, but they repay your debt and provide you with enough of a stipend to live off while you're working for them."

This was interesting, he thought, and it could be helpful. It was too late for him to join a program like that, but it might be a good recommendation for one of his clients.

"It's not just AmeriCorps," she said. "There are a bunch of programs like that, where you can effectively work off the loan."

Jake had his notebook out and was writing this down. For the next twenty minutes, they talked about some of the different options. He was already thinking ahead. If someone seemed particularly interested in a volunteer opportunity, maybe Maya would be willing to do her own session with them—and, of course, she could then earn some of the fee. He made a note to add it to his list of resources.

It reminded him of something he'd been reading about student loan forbearance. Apparently there were lots of situations where you could defer making payments, with no major penalty and no negative effect on your credit score. The financial services firm that had purchased his debt and was now seeking collection hadn't said anything about that. He wanted to help people like him make their debt disappear, not just go away for a while, but again, it was good to know that there were options.

They'd been at the Lava Java for nearly two hours. As much as Jake enjoyed seeing her, he didn't want to prolong the visit too much.

"So . . . maybe we can do this again sometime?" he asked.

"Of course," she said. "But just one thing. I have a lot to think about right now, so can we focus on being friends?"

He had no idea what that meant.

"Sure," he said. "And hey, no stress about this weekend. Right now I'm not even sure if I'll have a place."

They walked back to her car before saying goodbye. He couldn't tell what she was thinking, and he still had many of the same problems he did the day before.

Even so, he felt he'd made progress. And no matter what happened with them next—to use Maya's expression from the email—he knew he'd done the right thing and stepped up.

34.

The next day, Jake woke up excited. It was the day he would sign a new lease and begin to move back into a real apartment, a project that had been on hold while he was figuring out how to pay for it. Before the day ended, however, his celebratory mood would vanish, and his housing troubles were the last thing on his mind.

What was perhaps the most pressing of the problems that had begun a month before was now solved. The new apartment was smaller than his last one, but it suited him just fine. He now had fewer boxes to move, since he'd shipped out all his old textbooks and half of an extensive video game collection that he'd held on to for a decade. Then, of course, the flood had conveniently ruined all of his towels and most of the laundry that was in the hamper.

He put some groceries on the counter and turned back to grab a few boxes from the car. Later on he'd move over the rest of the stuff he'd been keeping at the office. Maybe he'd give Romeo George a call to see if he knew a furniture guy.

As he was unpacking, trying to decide where to place his desk, thinking that he really should put up those groceries, he received some news that made everything else completely irrelevant.

It arrived in a phone call from an unknown number, which he ignored at first. *Must be telemarketers.*

When he didn't pick up, he heard another ping with a message. "Jake, it's Celia from the group. I got your number from Preena. Can you call me back ASAP?"

He called her right away. "Celia? Hey, how are you and how are things with your web—"

She cut him off. "Jake, listen. Where are you now?"

"Uh . . . I'm at my apartment. I just got a new place and I'm un—"

"Some of us are at the hospital. Can you come right now?"

The hospital?

"Sure, yeah, of course. But what's going on . . . are you alright?"

"It's Clarence," she said. "He's had some kind of heart attack."

Act III

35.

At least Clarence was at the hospital, Jake thought as he threw on his shoes and raced to the car. Hospitals had doctors. They could hook you up to those machines. They could use that thing—a defibrillator?—to bring you back to consciousness.

Later on, they'd all talk about how scary it was, how it gave them perspective. "We almost lost you, Clarence," they'd say. "We were really worried for a while."

Clarence would need time to recover. He'd have to switch to decaf, no doubt grumbling with every cup he made.

But that's not how life works, is it? We don't get to decide whether an emergency is a close call or the close of a chapter.

Shaking himself out of the daydream, Jake arrived at the hospital, illegally parking the Mazda in front of a dumpster because he wasn't about to circle the block waiting for a space.

"What happened?" he asked breathlessly as he entered the emergency room. Adrian and Celia were already there, sitting in the corner next to an untouched stack of old magazines.

"We don't really know," Adrian said. "Someone is going to explain . . . something. Right now we're just waiting."

"You were just with him in Africa, right?" Celia asked.

"Yeah . . . three days ago."

He'd dropped Jake off and driven away. What had they said to each other then? He tried to remember every word.

A few minutes later, a young resident came out to speak with them. "Are you the family of Clarence Johnson?"

"We're not family," Adrian said, "but he means a lot to us. We've been trying to reach his ex-wife to see who else we should contact."

"Very well," the man said. "Let me tell you what we know so far. First, my name is Dr. Banerjee. I was on duty when your friend came in.

"He suffered from an acute myocardial infarction, more commonly known as a heart attack. By the time he arrived at the emergency room, he had been experiencing cerebral hypoxia, a lack of oxygen to the brain, for close to ten minutes. At that point, death is almost always imminent. In fact, after around five minutes, the best-case scenario is that the patient will stabilize into a coma with extensive brain damage.

"Mr. Johnson had a DNR order on file from his primary doctor, meaning that he wished to not be resuscitated should an incident like this occur. Your friend died a few minutes after he was transferred to the ER."

They were all struggling to take in the news.

"There's one more thing," the doctor said, reviewing his notes. "I noticed that he had a condition known as Barlow's syndrome that essentially foretold this outcome."

"*What?*" All three of them asked the question at once.

"The medical term is mitral valve prolapse. It means that one or more of the valves between his heart's chambers never properly closed. Basically, his heart wasn't operating correctly. As a consequence, he was more likely to have this kind of acute incident, and less likely to hold up to it. That's why it happened so quickly. Frankly, most people with the diagnosis don't live as long as he did."

This was even more to take in.

"How long had he known about . . . the condition?" Jake finally asked.

"For most of his adult life, as far as we can tell. It looks like he was first diagnosed around age twenty-three. He took regular medication, but from what I can see it doesn't look like he curbed his activities or held back on anything he wanted to do." He studied the chart again. "Recently he'd been going to a specialist in Seattle, but it looks like that was more for tests and research than treatment. I suspect he wanted to contribute however he could to anyone else with the condition in the future. For him, it seems it was just a matter of time. Again, I'm so sorry."

Dr. Banerjee waited respectfully.

"Thank you, Doctor," Celia said after a long pause. "We appreciate you doing what you could."

"Of course," he said. He shook their hands and walked out of
the reception area.

For a long time they just stood there, saying nothing.

36.

What they finally did was gather at Jake's new apartment. He wasn't prepared to host, but no one had been prepared for the news they'd all heard.

"Make yourselves at home . . . or on the floor, I guess." He went back out to the car and brought in a couple of cushions and pillows from the trunk.

The grocery bags he'd left on the counter four hours earlier contained a six-pack of warm beer and a carton of spoiled milk. At least he'd brought over a few water cups, which he filled and handed out after putting the beers in the fridge.

Preena came by, and then Jo and Adrian. Keisha called in from a new nursing assignment she'd just started in Phoenix. Everyone had questions that had no good answers.

Mostly they all just sat there. Nobody knew what to say or do, but it felt better to be together.

The next night, several of them met up again. By then, Jake had tracked down Clarence's lawyer, and Celia had found his ex-wife, Maria. Getting everyone together on a conference call couldn't solve the unsolvable, but at least they had something to do.

The lawyer was taking the lead on coordinating plans for the funeral. In the meantime, they began to fill in some more gaps in the story.

———

Clarence had been in the navy for five years before his heart condition was diagnosed. His request for a medical waiver was denied on the grounds that it was too risky, especially since the navy had a habit of being out at sea for long periods of time. Honorably discharged, he moved to Maryland for a while before drifting back to California, where he'd done much of his naval training.

Over time, he began to view his discharge as a blessing in disguise. After briefly working a sales job, he started a series of ventures, applying his phone card reselling skills to other markets. Somewhere along the way, he took a trip to Honduras and fell in love with coffee. He thought about starting his own roasting supplier, but decided it wasn't the right business for him.

Maria said later that they'd married too young, right before he'd gone off to another of his deployments. Once they were around each other all the time, she realized she wanted a different life. They divorced amicably and she eventually remarried. They continued to keep in touch from time to time, and in the past few years he'd started sending Christmas cards to her new family.

After splitting up with Maria, Clarence took stock of his life and decided he needed another change. That was when he started more than a phone card hustle. He built a *company*.

The company provided database services to government agencies. He'd been trained in operations in the navy and had seen up close how complex the logistics could be for storing and moving thousands of shipping containers around the world. His service would provide detailed projections for optimizing the process, potentially saving a great deal of time and money if the recommendations were followed.

He also took care to hire smart people. Since he wasn't a programmer himself, he looked for highly competent tech staff who could make sure the company was providing the best possible service.

He called the business ShipShape. The company got its first military contract for $5 million, and Clarence leased a suite of offices in Huntington Beach. The scope of the contract increased the following year, bringing in more revenue and requiring additional staff to meet all the demands for deliverables. All told, they had close to thirty employees at the peak.

They also had just one customer, the U.S. government. This fact made for an easy job in the accounts receivable department, but an uneasy feeling among several of the managers. They all agreed it was important to diversify, but with the money coming in every quarter, and no shortage of work to do for their one big contract, it was hard to think about the future.

Besides, the contract was renewed year after year without fail. Government work might be boring, but it was always dependable.

Or so they thought. With little warning, ShipShape received a letter stating that the contract wouldn't be renewed when it ended in sixty days. Upon asking around, they learned that a newer company had been awarded the job. The fact that the father of the other company's CEO had close connections to one of California's U.S. senators had nothing to do with the decision, they were told.

Panic ensued. They tried to sign other contracts, but making deals with the government required a long lead time and a lot of patience. In a last-ditch effort, they attempted to change direction by offering the service to the private sector. It might have worked if they'd started earlier, but solutions built for government are different from those for the marketplace. And without a dedicated sales team, they didn't get far.

Clarence's employees were loyal. They didn't blame him for the company's downfall, but he blamed himself. He knew in his heart that at least some of them expected him to solve the problem. They had trusted him enough to buy into his vision. He would take care of them, right?

More than anything, he wanted to. But there was no magic way to meet payroll without income, and no bank would lend money to a business without customers. After four years of steady profits, the business closed less than three months after the big contract ended.

Everyone was laid off, including several employees with families who had left other jobs and moved across the country to join the company. Six months before the end, one particularly talented programmer had been headhunted for a position at a small but promising company in Redmond, Washington, called Microsoft. He turned it down to work for ShipShape.

Clarence retreated, moving to Texas and taking a job as a midlevel executive with an oil company that did geomapping. His knowledge of government contracts was valuable, but he disliked the rituals of office politics that were required to move up in that world. In his second year there, he started another business on the side.

By his fifth year, he'd started two more side businesses, and he finally quit his job to go all in. This time, he was far more intentional with growth. He hired only when he felt confident he could support the new employees. Most of the time, he didn't hire at all—he contracted for the services he needed, making certain he wouldn't extend an offer he might not be able to fulfill. He didn't rely on a single project for his income, and he spent as much time working on the underlying systems of the business as he did trying to generate sales.

After ten years, he "retired," moving back to California and no longer actively starting projects but continuing to earn passive income from the earlier ones. He started teaching the Third Way model, not in a flashy way and never trying to make a name for himself. He never wrote a book or went on the speaking circuit. He just began *helping people.*

He paid for his housekeeper's son to go to college, even though the woman came by only once a week and he hadn't known her for long. He did as much for his former employees as possible, providing glowing references when they changed jobs and teaching some of them how to make money on their own.

Later, the stories poured in. There were dozens . . . hundreds . . . the group lost count. Many people noted that he'd asked them to keep his involvement private. He truly seemed motivated to do all he could, for however much time he had left.

It had been fifteen years since his company closed and he set out on his second act, but in the piecing together of the story, it seemed short. Meanwhile, it had been twenty-four hours since his death, and it felt much longer.

By now, the news of Clarence's fatal heart attack was getting around. An online memorial page went up and was quickly filled with a stream of heartfelt comments. The funeral would be held in five days. Judging by what people were sharing on the page, it seemed that many of them would be traveling in for it.

When Jake had spoken with the lawyer, he learned that Clarence had made detailed plans for this occasion. He'd even prepaid the expenses for a ceremony. The lawyer said that Clarence had asked that someone from the Third Way group be invited to speak at the funeral. Could Jake ask around and see if anyone would be up for it?

The group's vote was unanimous: *he* should do it. He began to protest, saying that he was the newest member—they had all known him much longer—but even as he did, he, too, felt that it was right. This was something he needed to do.

By the time everyone left that night, he was already thinking of what he might say.

37.

Work at Brightside wouldn't pause for a long grieving process. Jake had already taken time off for the trip, and would take another day for the funeral, so he had to show up at all other possible times.

Now, just two days after receiving the devastating news, he was back in the conference room, together with the rest of the team. He and Preena had agreed to not talk about what they were going through with anyone else at work, at least not right away.

"Okay, everyone, let's review where we're at." Marcie, the HR rep from the Philadelphia office, was on speakerphone, providing an update to the group.

Jake braced himself for the latest reprimand. They were here for an update on the assessment scores, and he'd been away for a week. He also wasn't sure what would happen with his big idea for the record label. What seemed brilliant in the middle of the night now felt a lot more questionable.

"So, let's see . . . who all is in the room? . . . Okay, Preena, Sloan, it looks like you two have been fairly steady. The system views you as competent and serving the company well."

They both looked relieved.

"Jake, I'm looking for your notes . . ."

Here it comes, he thought.

"Wow," Marcie said. "It looks like you've had quite a change for the better. In fact, the system shows that you're now ranking as one of the best-performing employees in the whole—"

Sloan broke in. "But that's impossible!" he complained, lowering his voice when he realized he was nearly shouting. "He hasn't even been here most of the time."

"The system automatically accounts for time away," she replied. "We can't penalize people for taking their normal vacation days. So in other words, it's just looking at the time in which he's been around."

Sloan slumped in his chair and looked offended, as if the idea that Jake's personal time belonged to him was outrageous. Jake was reminded of the time that their colleague Tami had a baby. Sloan was shocked to learn that her maternity leave would last more than a few days.

Marcie resumed her report to the group. "So that leaves Jan.

One sec while I pull up the whole report . . . okay, yeah, Jan, I'm sorry, but it looks like your assessment score is now at the bottom of the group."

Huh? That didn't sound right.

Preena spoke up first. "How could Jan's score be at the bottom? She's a great boss!"

"It's really all about ROI," Marcie explained. "That's what Dirk wants us to base all outcomes on—things like billable hours, new business, and upsells to clients."

Dirk Vanderpleitz was Magnate's CEO, who would soon be descending from the mountaintop to visit their office. ROI was *return on investment*, a measurement of which actions had the most impact on the bottom line.

"It really would help if we understood more about how this tool was grading us," Jan said. "I think I'm a pretty hard worker, and I want to support the company however I can."

"Again, it's all about ROI," came the reply from the speakerphone. "It looks like you spent several hours out of the office last week that didn't count as vacation and weren't accounted for."

"Oh," said Jan. "Well, my assistant, Lydia, had the flu, and she lives by herself. I knew she wouldn't miss three straight days of work unless it was really bad, so I went to her house to check in on her. When I arrived, it was clear that she needed help. I did some laundry for her, and went back to the grocery store to pick up some supplies. Then, the next day I returned to check in again."

"That could be it," Marcie replied. "Unfortunately we don't

really have a way to include things like that in the model. And like I said, Dirk wants the model to focus entirely around ROI."

Jake raised his hand, then realized that Marcie couldn't see him. He moved closer to the phone.

"Hey, Marcie, it's Jake. I have a question. Can *everything* be measured by this all-ROI-all-the-time model?"

She paused. "Well, why not? You know the saying that we sometimes pass on to clients: what's measured gets done."

"I agree that's a good philosophy much of the time," Jake said. "I just wonder if there are some pretty important exceptions. Jan looking out for her assistant's well-being, for example. Also," he continued, "what if I do something for an important client that's technically outside the scope of our contract, but turns out to be critical to their business? There's no financial return, since we can't charge for it, but isn't it good customer service? And doesn't it benefit us in the long term to be known for going above and beyond?"

Marcie seemed to struggle in responding to anything that wasn't outlined in an HR manual. Finally, she said, "You know, these are good questions"—meaning that she hated them. "Why don't you ask Dirk when he's out there next week?"

"Okay," Jake said. "Maybe I will. And just for the record, Preena's right. Jan is a great boss."

It was a notable moment, speaking up for his boss like that. His inspiration came from thinking about Clarence. Even though they'd never talked about corporate assessments, Jake felt certain that he would have a fundamental objection to any process that treated people like machines.

The minor insurrection connected to the other task on his mind, and for the rest of the day he was determined to prioritize that item above everything else. He had to figure out what to say for the funeral.

38.

Jake was nervous. He hadn't been to a lot of funerals and wasn't sure what to expect. He'd been told that a minister would facilitate the ceremony and a musician would play a few songs. After the service there would be a reception, and anyone who had a story about Clarence would be invited to share. For the service itself, though, there were just three speakers: a friend from the navy, a former employee, and him.

Based on all the calls the funeral director had been receiving, they were expecting a full house.

The past few days had felt hopeless. Jake carried out the motions of life and work, but with a sense of deep sadness. Now, though, he tried to put his feelings on hold and think about what would be important to say. He needed to do a good job in honoring Clarence. It was, he realized, his last assignment.

He wrote down a few lines in his journal, crossed them out, and wrote a few more. He moved to his laptop, thinking that typing might be easier. But all that happened was that instead of crossing out his false starts, he held down the backspace key to make them vanish.

By the time an hour had passed, he'd started and stopped and started over half a dozen times. This was hard!

He closed his eyes and thought back on the trip they'd just taken. Did Clarence know then that his death was imminent? He knew that something was wrong with his heart, of course—that was why he was going back and forth to Seattle. But did he expect that something would happen soon?

There was no way to know for sure, but as he thought about it, Jake developed a working theory.

It's not that he knew it would happen "soon." It was that he knew it could happen at any time.

The last few months of his life weren't an attempt to cross off a bunch of bucket list items or reach out to anyone from the past to make amends. Instead, Clarence had simply resolved to focus his efforts on the people and projects that were important to him. Whatever time he had left, whether a week or a decade, was a gift.

The trip they'd taken would have been highly memorable even without the tragedy that followed. The time Jake had spent in the village, hanging out with Yonas, meeting Eshe, seeing all the roving vendors . . . it had affected him deeply.

He thought about meeting Clarence at the coffee shop, where he was waiting for Jake with a cup in his outstretched hand. Then for their second meeting, he took time to meet Jake early in the morning before dashing to Seattle for another round of tests.

Jake had sometimes been frustrated when Clarence wouldn't answer his questions or tell him exactly what to do, but he knew even then that he would probably learn more in the long run if he worked things out on his own. He just didn't know that he'd be on his own so soon.

When they returned from the big trip, he watched Clarence drive away for the last time. It was a weird sensation to realize that those words he'd said were the last they'd ever share.

What did he say, exactly?

"I was glad to have you there," he'd said, in response to Jake's expression of thanks. "You're on to something, Jake. And don't forget, you can do more than you think."

There was something affirming about nearly everything he said. Jake wanted to capture the essence of these conversations in a way that reflected the admiration he felt.

With all of that in mind, he started writing. Preparing this talk was like getting in the zone to work on his auction listings or brainstorming his service business ideas.

Except, of course, this was ultimately more important. He had only one chance to get it right.

39.

At two p.m. the next day, Jake found himself sitting in a large reception hall. Maya had taken off work to join him, and the entire Third Way group was sitting in two of the rows close to the front.

But it wasn't just them, of course. The place was packed. Anyone who glanced across the crowd would be impressed. All of these people, many of whom were entirely unknown to each other, were all linked to the life they were gathered to memorialize.

Jake had made careful notes on what he wanted to say, but he kept revising them throughout the morning. He tried to listen to the other speakers, especially a woman whom Clarence had helped start a business designing and importing textiles. The business now employed a dozen people, and she announced that she was beginning a scholarship fund in his name.

The details escaped his attention as he mentally rehearsed what he would say when it was his turn. A few minutes later, Jake approached the podium and looked out at the crowd.

The time had come.

"Good afternoon, everyone. I'm not surprised to see so many people here. I hope Clarence would appreciate such a good crowd showing up today. Although"—he paused for effect—"I'm pretty sure he would have hated the coffee. That stuff they're serving in the back is terrible!"

It was a gamble, leading with a joke, but it got a good laugh.

It was also just what he needed. He felt his shoulders relax and his jaw loosen. *The hardest part is starting,* he thought, *and that part is over.*

"In a lot of ways, I think I'm probably the least qualified person in the room to speak here. Most of you knew Clarence for years. I just met him very recently. So I look forward to hearing the stories later at the . . . reception."

He almost called it the afterparty. Who knows, maybe that would have gotten a laugh, too. He decided to not second-guess himself as much as he went along.

"Since I can't do justice to his entire biography, or speak about Clarence in the way that some of you might be able to, I thought I'd just tell a story from my perspective as someone new to his world— and I'll keep it short, because you're not here to hear about me.

"Some of you know that I traveled with Clarence on his last trip abroad. Between the flights and the time in Ethiopia, we got to spend a whole week together. Before that, even though I hadn't known him long, he had already affected my life quite a bit.

"It started when he gave me a challenge to make $1,000 in just a few days. At first, I was a little deflated, because what he told me to do didn't sound that groundbreaking. He also didn't tell me *how* to do it, which was frustrating at first. But I was pretty desperate, so I decided to try. Long story short, it worked!

"Earning the money was great, but it also made a big difference for my state of mind. I realized that I wasn't powerless. Even if circumstances were difficult, or if I'd made mistakes—I could figure it out and regroup."

From what he could tell from his perch in the front, the audience was following along closely. *So far, so good.*

"So that in itself was incredible. Honestly, I would have been thrilled if that was the extent of it. But then, like I said, I got the chance to travel with him on his final journey to Africa. I had no idea what to expect, and it all happened really fast—but that trip *also* ended up changing my life.

"I'm pretty sure I learned more in five days on the ground there than however much time I've spent anywhere else. In fact, the other night I tried to make a list of all the things I've learned from Clarence. I easily filled up the page and started on another. He taught me all about what makes for a good business idea. He showed me how there was something I could tap into that would help other people, while helping me at the same time. And through the group he started"—he nodded at them—"I learned a lot about how to communicate the benefits of an offer, how to start a service, and how to avoid getting sidetracked by a bunch of stuff that doesn't matter.

"But as amazing as all of that is, I realized that I actually learned something even more valuable." As he moved to the last page of his notes, Jake began to feel emotional. *Keep going,* he told himself. *Don't hold back. Give everything you can.*

"The honest truth is that because of the work I've done so far, I've gained a tremendous amount of self-confidence. I've thought a lot about the last thing he said to me. It didn't seem like a final farewell—he was just dropping me back at the office after we returned from the trip. But even then, he left me feeling like I was on the right track with my life. I was excited to keep exploring the Third Way model, and I looked forward to whatever came next.

"For me, that's what it comes down to. Because of Clarence, and the legacy that he lived in service to others, I began to believe in myself. There's no way to tell you how important this is, but I wanted to acknowledge it here publicly, in front of all of you who have also benefited from knowing him."

He'd been glancing at his notes every few seconds, but now he covered up the papers and looked directly at the audience.

"There's just one more thing I'd like to say—and again, I know most of you knew him better than me, so I don't want to overstep my role. But when I was thinking about how to prepare for today, I was *going* to say something about how I have no idea how to repay the debt I owe him.

"Then I realized that wasn't completely true. I *do* have a way to give back, or at least pay it forward. I think what he would want me to do, and not just me but maybe a lot of you as well, is to adopt some of his values as my own.

"Of course, I don't have the experience he did, and I haven't built a company—but I know that I can do *something* to help people. I also want to live the way he did, by appreciating each day and trying to get as much out of it as possible."

Jake paused before his concluding statement, looking around the room one more time.

"I think Clarence would have wanted us to live for something, and that's what I'm going to do. Thank you, everyone."

He walked away from the podium and sat down. Maya squeezed his hand. At least for a few moments, he felt relieved. More than anything, he had wanted to use those few minutes well, and he felt that he had.

Then the service continued and he noticed he was crying. He realized he'd been looking to the talk as some kind of continuation of his relationship with Clarence. As long as the task was still on the horizon, it was as though his mentor and friend wasn't really gone.

But now the talk was over, the task complete, and there was

nothing else he could do. After today, he'd return to a world that was forever changed. Life would resume, he would go to the office, he would work on his business. Just not in the same way.

There was no looking back. All he could do was move forward.

All he could do was live for something, like he'd just promised to do.

40.

From: KQuanChangi97@robomail.com
To: IT
CC: Inner Circle

Good morning! I'm having a hard time logging into my Buzzmail. Can you wave your magic wand or whatever you do to get it working again? In the meantime I'm available here if anyone needs me.

———

From: Kevin Quan
To: All Users

Attention Buzzard-ites: when your fearless founder said your decisions were out of your hands, he wasn't kidding.

As of this morning, he is no longer in charge. We're currently digging through all your emails to see what might be of interest.

The only way to stop our invasion is by paying a ransom. Tick-tock, the clock is winding down . . .

———

From: KQuanChangi97@robomail.com
To: Inner Circle
WTF was that!! I did NOT send that message.

———

From: KQuanChangi97@robomall.com
To: All Users
Valued Buzzers,

Everyone, I'm so sorry—that last message didn't come from me. It appears we've been hacked, and our crack IT team is looking at it right now. (I'm not saying they're on crack, ha!)

Don't worry, your data is completely safe.

Remaining vigilant,

The Real Kevin

———

From: Kevin Quan
To: All Users
Actually, this is the real Kevin Quan. Or is it? When you think about it, how do you know if anything's real anymore?

Here's the deal: We have taken over the mainframe of this ridiculous company. If our demands aren't met, we will begin distributing any private photos found in your email or messaging accounts.

Your favorite founder, CEO, and COO has 60 minutes to comply.

Don't worry, it's for your own good.

Breaking: Controversial Decision-Making Service Under Attack

Reuters Newswire

—

Sources indicate a new service that advises users on their decisions has been hacked.

More than 250,000 users have allowed the service to access their personal information, including email and financial accounts. There is no word yet as to whether those accounts are at risk.

This is a developing story and will be updated.

From: KQuanChangi97@robomail.com
To: lolzhackbuzz@hushmail.com
What is Ethereum? And why would I pay you $100,000?
Who are you?

But What Could Possibly Go Wrong?

By Katlyn Everett

Valley News

Pop quiz time again!

Who plays with fire and acts surprised when their house burns down? Ding ding! You guessed it . . . Buzzard Co., that's who.

The popular "do no good" startup is *shocked* that they would be a target for hackers. They are *horrified* at such maliciousness. They are *doing everything they can* to regain access to their systems.

Is your data safe? In the words of its ever-quotable founder, "Ha!"

That appears to be an open question, as the founder no longer has access to his own email account. Additionally, the home page of BuzzardCo .com currently features an image of a skeleton holding a set of car keys. While I would not be surprised if this emerged as its new logo, for now it seems to be an action taken by the hackers.

There's a good reason why messages that delete themselves upon being viewed are so popular.

Stay tuned for updates on the house burning. I'm running out to get popcorn.

———

From: KQuanChangi97@robomail.com
To: Finance
How do I transfer a large amount of money? And do you know what Ethereum is??

———

UPDATED: Decision-Making Service Resolves Attempted Hacking

Reuters Newswire

—

The concern that hackers had gained control of a startup's full set of user accounts turned into a false alarm.

Users breathed a sigh of relief as experts learned that only the service's home page and founder's email account had been compromised. He regained access after paying the hackers an undisclosed sum in the form of a ransom payment.

In an embarrassing moment, it was revealed that the password used to access his account was "1234567890."

Consider it a reminder to use better passwords than startup CEOs do.

———

From: Kevin Quan
To: IT
Ugh. I was going to change it!
I tried one of those longer passwords for a while, but it had a bunch of weird characters and was hard to remember.

———

From: Kevin Quan
To: Inner Circle
What a day it's been! I'm trying to get us back on track here . . . we need to regain the momentum.
In other news, why do we have so many Buzz shirts left

over? I'm stepping over boxes everywhere I go. I guess we estimated a little high.

———

From: Kevin Quan

To: All Users

We are back up!!! Yes, it's me—the Official Kevin Quan!

I'm sorry about this morning, and I very much appreciate your faith in us.

But we're also in trouble. As the financial wizards say, our coffers are runnin' low. Can you help?

For a limited time, we're offering a special bonus in our owner-investor program. For a deposit of just $1,000, we'll send you a high-quality T-shirt featuring the Buzzard logo. You'll be the fashion hit of your office!

Bring back the buzz!!

Safety first,

Kevin Quan

———

From: Kevin Quan

To: Finance; PR

I just saw the news. We should clarify that an SEC investigation is totally normal.

I think something like "We welcome the investigation to demonstrate how secure our systems are . . ." could be a good approach. Thoughts??

———

From: Kevin Quan
To: Zach Aarons
A corporate-giving initiative is a great idea. It could get the focus off the data breach and back to our core values of helping people.

I know just the thing. Stay tuned.

———

From: Kevin Quan
To: Gloria Armstrong, Guiding Light Ministries
Dear Gloria,

Allow me to introduce myself. I'm the Founder, CEO, and COO of Buzzard Co., a new network that is out to change the world. As part of our efforts, we want to make sure we don't neglect our neighbors right here in Emeryville!

I understand that your organization provides care and housing for homeless persons in the area. We would like to make a considerable donation of several hundred T-shirts, emblazoned with the beautiful Buzzard logo. These shirts are sure to brighten up anyone's day, even when they're down on their luck.

Giving is in our DNA, and I don't want to make a big deal about this. A few TV cameras and a small media event would be fine. Can we plan to come by next Tuesday?

In service,

Kevin Quan

———

From: Kevin Quan

To: Gloria Armstrong

I'm glad to know you've heard of us! Although I'm sorry that your friends were spamming you with referral links last week.

I also appreciate your feedback about the donation. I would have thought the shirts would be a highly valuable contribution on their own. They are high quality and printed on 100% cotton. However, we can agree to your request to provide a cash donation in addition to the shirts. Can we still plan on Tuesday afternoon?

By the way, it would be good to have some homeless persons in attendance for the media event. I'd love to meet a few of your customers who will be sporting new clothes on Wednesday!

Your new donor,

Kevin Quan

———

From: Kevin Quan

To: Inner Circle

She wants a cash donation . . . apparently they're concerned about it being more of a photo op than a real contribution. I told her we could figure something out.

———

—Three Days Later—

From: Kevin Quan

To: All Staff

I hope you all had a good weekend! We're in recovery mode, but we're going to pull through.

I've been thinking that it would be good for us to do something to give back. Accordingly, I've arranged to make a substantial donation to a local charity that serves the homeless. As part of the event, I should be appearing on the news tomorrow night—be sure to tune in online and spread the buzz love!

Let's work together to build a kinder and gentler Buzzard. We WILL make it!

To the Buzz,

Kevin

———

From: Kevin Quan

To: Hilary Hodgkins; Zach Aarons

I'm attaching a draft of my speech for the event. What do you guys think? All comments are welcome—don't hold back!

———

From: Kevin Quan

To: Hilary Hodgkins

Wow, that's harsh. Personally I think the talk is really strong. I also don't see your point about how it could be misconstrued. Still, I'll take your critiques under consideration.

T-minus four hours to showtime!

———

KEYNOTE ADDRESS TO GUIDING LIGHT

Tap, tap . . . is this on? Can you hear me out there?

Community leaders, representatives of the media, and homeless persons:

At Buzzard Co., we spend our days helping users make important decisions about their lives. No matter what the critics say about us, we're proud of what we do. Yet it's also very important to give back to our local community. We stand with you. We see you!

When it came time to ask, "What can we offer people in need of a fresh start in life?" the answer came back loud and clear: *T-shirts.* We had a bunch of extras that were taking up space, and as we can see today, the homeless population needs to be clothed.

To the media representatives here, we all know that it's easy to be cynical. There are so many challenges in the world these days. Yet if you look around the room, you can see the evidence of our generosity for yourselves. It's my hope that you'll feature this event in prime coverage as a counterexample to every story about war or deforestation.

And to those homeless persons in attendance today, we hope this donation will set you on a path to a better life. Perhaps one day in the future, you'll look back and view this afternoon as the moment that changed everything.

Lastly, I regret that we don't have a lot of sizing options for the shirts. If your size isn't available, please choose the next closest one.

Thank you, everyone.

———

From: Zach Aarons

To: Jake Aarons

Hey man, not sure if you've seen the news lately. Buzzard is a sinking ship, and I need a lifeline. Can you explain more about this reselling thing you're doing?

41.

Jake settled back into his normal life as best he could. After a month of extreme highs and lows, where time seemed to operate in a vortex, now everything felt slow. He got up, he went to work, he went home. Throughout the day, he felt the absence of his friend and mentor.

In better news, Student Loan Champion was humming along. Several new inquiries came from a podcast he'd been mentioned in. There wasn't a flood of customers crashing his site with enthusiasm, but every day or two, his phone would chirp with the notice of an incoming payment. It felt good.

He thought about something Clarence had said. *Focus on what's in front of you. Once you have customers or clients, spend your time thinking about how you can best serve them. Don't just think about how you can get "more."*

Focus on what's in front of you: he was getting better at that part at least, in more ways than one.

Until something happened that threatened to sabotage the whole project.

He'd signed up for a free news alert that would ping him whenever his business was mentioned somewhere online. He thought it might be useful in the future. For now, the whole thing was an exercise in ego management. He'd been signed up for two weeks, and so far he'd had a grand total of . . . two pings. One was from that podcast, and another was from a blogger who had linked to his site as a resource for her readers.

The third ping arrived when he was in a meeting. He was doing his best to separate the day job from the side business, but he couldn't help taking a quick peek at the notification. What he saw caused him to worry—a lot.

He tried to remain calm for the rest of the meeting before dashing back to his desk and pulling it up again. The notification read:

Student Loan Champion is a scam! Save your money.

What in the world?

He clicked the link and saw it led to a forum consisting of anonymous reviews about various businesses. The forum seemed to serve as an outpost of negativity, with little moderation and a criticism-to-praise ratio of at least 10:1.

But why would his brand-new service be included here? As he continued to read, he had a sinking feeling. Somehow, it seemed that someone had been upset and left him a highly negative review.

He realized right away how damaging this could be. Sure, no one but him had news alerts set up for his business, but the review site had been around a long time and had thousands of pages. He could tell from a glance that it probably ranked well in search results— meaning that when anyone searched "Student Loan Champion," the odds were that they'd see this page and its title ("Student Loan Champion is a scam!") near the top.

Not quite the first impression he was hoping for.

He read through the post and became even more concerned. Many of the other reviews were poorly written, with an excessive number of exclamation points, and an average of two grammatical errors per sentence. A typical complaint would drag on for several paragraphs, often devolving into rants that had nothing to do with the company in question. Jake's interpretation was that most reasonable people wouldn't be put off by them.

The review about his service, however, was different. It was hard-hitting, specific, and succinct.

> I hired Student Loan Champion to help me, and the founder ripped me off. The website promised to teach me a skill, but I didn't know the skill would be picking my own pocket. After paying the outrageous $150 fee, I was never contacted by anyone. Now I STILL have my debt, AND I've lost $150. Stay away!!

Seriously—what in the world?

This was damaging stuff. And it was completely untrue—but no one else knew that. If he'd stumbled on the review while checking out his own service, he'd hesitate before signing up for it.

From what he could tell, most people who used the forum operated from the assumption that all businesses were run by evil villains and that every complaint had built-in credibility. The post had already received a couple dozen "thumbs-up" emoji responses, and the only reply was complimentary. ("Thank you for sharing this . . . it sounds like a completely fraudulent operation! I hope they get shut down.") No one questioned the review's truthfulness.

Jake forced himself to slow down and think. Who would do this, and on what basis could they possibly complain?

He thought back to a few days ago. It was his first doubleheader, where he landed two new clients in a day. He celebrated by buying his coffee from the hipster shop across from the office. In honor of Clarence, he was learning about different kinds of fair trade roasts.

Taking a short break to clear his head was good. Besides, he was never going to get out of debt by saving $4 a day.

He scheduled the first call with Jamal, a recent graduate from Michigan who had a lot of initiative. Even as an entry-level engineer, Jamal was earning a high salary—and he wanted to put as much of it as possible toward paying off his loans.

The second client had paid but not scheduled—which seemed odd, since the scheduling page appeared right after making a purchase. Still, Jake figured they might have gotten distracted some-where. It certainly happened to him often enough.

Every other client interaction he'd had so far was extremely pos-itive. If the forum post really was from a real customer, it had to be this person.

Maybe it was all a big misunderstanding?

That seemed unlikely, but Jake pulled up the customer's email address and sent a quick note just in case. He tried to keep it light—after all, he wasn't sure this was the same person who'd trashed his reputation on the forum.

Twenty seconds after sending the message, he had a reply. Sort of.

> Your message cannot be delivered. Please check the recipient's details and try again.

Huh. Jake double-checked to make sure he hadn't made a typo, but that was hard to do when using copy-and-paste.

While he was trying to decide what to do next, his phone chirped with a notification from the bank. Another sale!

Well, that's good. At least the word about my fraudulent business hasn't gotten out yet.

Or maybe it had, because this sale notification looked different from all the others. It was more like . . . a reverse sale. Jake read it with increasing distress. Instead of receiving $150, his account had been *debited* $180. When he clicked through to see the full mes-sage, his discomfort ratcheted up even further.

A customer has filed a dispute regarding a recent purchase.
We have debited your account for the amount of the
purchase, in addition to a $30 chargeback fee.

Debited his account? A *chargeback fee?* It seemed his new business
was now earning negative money. This wasn't exactly what he had
in mind when he decided to get out of debt.

42.

Jake pushed back his chair and went for a walk around the block. He'd received a complaint, a bad review, and something called a "chargeback" all in one day. Clarence hadn't taught him anything about how to handle this.

The rest of the notice from the bank explained that he could challenge the dispute by providing documentation, and the credit card company would review the info that both sides submitted. Sixty to ninety days later, or whenever they got around to it, they would let him know what they decided.

It also noted that the bank's compliance department was closely monitoring every merchant's activity. Any merchants with charge-backs were at risk of being cut off—they would simply lose the ability to accept customer payments, with no notice, appeals process, or viable backup plan.

Jake was taken aback. A customer he'd had no interaction with had posted a highly negative review about him, in a source that was likely to show up whenever anyone searched for his business. Then they'd gone to their credit card company and filed a complaint, which resulted in the charge being reversed and a fee added to his account—and worst of all, the threat of being cut off from future payments.

Through applying the Third Way model, Jake had learned that making even small amounts of money could feel disproportionately satisfying. Every $150 payment he received felt like much more. Now he learned something else: *losing* $150—or actually, $180—felt truly heart-wrenching.

With the email address bouncing back, he had no idea how to find the mystery buyer. Thinking quickly, he dialed the number included in the bank's notice. After fifteen minutes of being transferred around, he reached the compliance department. Before he could finish explaining the situation, the rep cut him off.

"I won't be able to give you any more information than you already have, Mr. Aarons," she told him. "We take complaints from our cardholders very seriously."

"Okay, sure," he said. "But what if the customer is a ghost? What if it's someone who buys a consultation, doesn't schedule an appointment, and then files a complaint right away? That's just not fair."

"We can't give you any more infor—" she began again.

"Alright, fine. I'll figure something out." He hung up and walked back inside.

That was a dead end. What would Zach do in this situation?

He'd been thinking more about his brother ever since they'd talked after the funeral. They often texted throughout the day, sharing short updates and photos. Zach was doing his best to rein in Kevin at Buzzard, and so far it was a losing battle. Jake could tell he'd become disillusioned with the startup model and was increasingly curious to learn about the Third Way. They were going to meet again soon to brainstorm an escape route.

Jake wrote to him now and shared a quick version of the story, including a screenshot of the review.

Zach replied right away. "That's crazy, bro. Have you checked the IP address of the bank charge?"

The what? Jake quickly searched online to see what an IP address was.

Hm. Every computer connected to the internet has a specific identifier.

You can use an IP address to find someone, or at least narrow down the candidates to a specific area. With a bit of effort it was possible to mask your IP address to be untraceable, but most people didn't know how or just didn't bother.

If every computer with an internet connection had an identifier, that meant that his did, too. He typed in another search phrase: "What is my IP address?"

He expected the search to lead to a complicated process. He'd need to explain to the people who ran the internet (there are such people, right?) why he wanted to look up his unique identifier. They'd probably charge a fee. Maybe they'd make him wait ninety days before deciding if they approved his request.

None of that happened. Instead, the result came back immediately. At the top of the search results, he had his answer.

> Your IP address is 184.183.163.215

Well, that was easy enough. But what could he do with this information? It was just a string of random numbers.

Zach had pulled a Clarence, dropping some Yoda-esque knowledge before disappearing. *Fear is the path to the dark side. But first, check the IP address you must.*

Discouraged, he started to get back to the latest research he was doing for Brightside. He really did need to focus on the job he was getting paid for, especially now that he was losing money at the other one.

But wait . . . Zach had said to check the IP address *of the bank charge*. How would he get that? The compliance rep at the bank wouldn't even confirm that the Earth was round.

He logged back into his bank account and looked at the order. It didn't tell him much that he didn't already know. But looking closer, he noticed that it did in fact include another set of random numbers that looked a lot like the ones he'd seen when he'd searched for his own.

Back in the other tab, he searched for another phrase: "IP address lookup." Then he copied and pasted the numbers from the order, expecting his computer to rise from the desk and give him a high five like the kids in the village had done.

His computer remained stubbornly in place. The IP address search just returned a bunch of other random numbers that didn't mean anything to him.

Where was Yoda when you needed him? *Much to learn, you still have.*

Then he looked again and noticed something very strange.

What the . . . wait, that can't be right.

He must have made a mistake somewhere. He went through the process once more and stared at the result.

What were the odds? It had to be in the millions.

He called Preena over and filled her in. "Are you seeing what I'm seeing?" he asked.

She looked at the order, then copied over the numbers herself. They both watched the result pop up on the screen. Then she opened a new window and typed in "What is my IP address?" again.

"That's so weird," she said.

The numbers were exactly the same.

It was straight out of a bad horror movie. They were hiding from a serial killer, who kept calling on the phone to taunt them . . . and then they realized *the calls were coming from inside the house.*

43.

That was bizarre, and before the week was over, a lot of things would get even stranger. But for now, Jake forced himself to make a mental shift and put off the investigation.

After returning from Ethiopia, he'd been working on a project even more important than Student Loan Champion. It had been on his mind ever since he received the unfortunate "Let's take a break" email six weeks earlier.

Instead of becoming sidetracked by the tragedy of losing Clarence, Jake was propelled by it. Just a few days back he'd spoken in front of several hundred people, telling them he was going to be brave and live for something. Today was an important step in putting actions to words.

At some point the project had grown into more of a mission, or what he thought of as a "special operation." He'd made careful preparations for this mission. He'd sketched a plan in his notebook, charting a course for the next several hours. He'd considered as many contingencies as possible, formulating backup plans and detours should they be required.

Of course, there were always uncertainties, the variables that couldn't be controlled or even predicted. But those were events he'd have to handle as they developed in real time. That was what special operations ultimately came down to.

He reviewed his resources. Enough cash in the wallet in the event of any surprise debit card rejections. Three granola bars in case snacks were needed. Preena on standby for emergency text message relationship advice.

In a true sign of his commitment to the cause, he even turned off his payment notifications. If anyone signed up for a loan consultation, he'd have to wait at least four hours before seeing it.

He called it Operation New Beginnings. The high-level exercise began at seven p.m.

———

"So," she said when he picked her up. "Where are we going?"

"Downtown!" he said. "I made a reservation at a place I think you'll like."

Jake tried to play it cool when Maya got in the car. She observed that the back of the Mazda looked a lot neater than when she saw it in the parking lot the week before. He agreed, noting that it was significantly easier to keep your car clean when you weren't living in it.

They drove into the city and Jake found a parking spot. Maya smiled in recognition when she saw their destination. "Jake, you hated this place," she said. "Didn't you?"

It was true. He wasn't a huge fan of the Thankful Bistro. Rather than lie, he tried to change the subject. "Did you see that the Warriors beat the Trail Blazers yesterday?"

"Not really," she laughed. "But seriously, thanks for bringing me here. We should go somewhere we both like next time."

Was it karma or dogma that resulted in Chyna being their server again? He always got those confused. She greeted them warmly, enthusing to Maya about a chakra healing retreat she'd been on.

Her arrival at the table might have thrown the old Jake. But this time, he was prepared to discuss his energy levels, smile in response to stupid questions, and—if absolutely necessary—even pretend to like her.

"Are we celebrating tonight?" Chyna asked with a wink as she handed out the menus.

"Yes," he answered. "We'd like a double portion of your most expensive lentils."

Maya kicked him under the table. From what he could tell, she did it playfully.

Twenty minutes later, with their real dinner orders placed and a sample platter of kale and carrots on the table, Jake began his second important speech of the week.

"So, Maya," he began. "Here's the thing. Over the past month I've had some time to think. A lot of time, actually, especially when I wasn't sleeping much. It's all felt like a blur, with one thing after another. Until all of this stuff happened, I felt like I was living on autopilot, just kind of going through the motions. I didn't put much effort toward the things that are truly important. Like you, for example. But wait, don't say anything just yet."

He was worried she'd cut him off before he could finish. No matter the outcome, he had to make his best client pitch.

"The whirlwind trip to Ethiopia really inspired me. I learned a lot, but I also *felt* something different. The last day I was there, I went for a run and remembered some dreams and goals I hadn't thought about in a long time."

The pitch was starting well. Maya had put down her carrot stick and was looking at him intently.

"Look, I know it's still early in our relationship, and I know my recent track record hasn't been the best, but . . ."

All of a sudden, Chyna had seemingly teleported next to them and was hovering over their table. "If I could suggest something—" she started to say.

Jake glared at her. *"Chyna, shut the f—"*

He didn't actually say that.

He smiled at her instead. "Chyna, could you please give us a couple of minutes?"

Even Maya seemed relieved when she walked away.

"Anyway, as I was saying . . ." He sat up straight. This time, he'd even practiced the ending. "You said you wanted some space, and that's totally cool. With everything that was happening with me a few weeks ago, I get it. And I also understand if that means you never want us to try dating again. But what I'm saying is that I'm willing to stick around as long as you want me to. You're one of the best things that's ever happened to me, so if you do decide you want to try again, you can count on me.

"Also, if I ever get flooded out of my apartment again, I promise to tell you. I even made sure to get renter's insurance this time! And I now carry a lot of cash in case my card is ever declined."

Maya laughed. "Jake, it wasn't a big deal to pick up the check that night. You know I don't expect you to always do that. What bothered me was that I didn't know what was going on, and it didn't seem like you wanted to include me."

He relaxed a little. "I know, it was the wrong decision. I think I was scared if you knew the whole story, you'd walk away."

"Well," she said. "I'm here now."

They sat there for a while longer. A chastened Chyna returned to offer dessert, which featured a special of dried beans and cilantro for just $18.

Jake looked at Maya. He was fully prepared to sell a textbook to pay for whatever expensive cardboard treat she wanted to try.

But that's not what she wanted. "Let's finish up here and go for ice cream," she said. "And then let's figure out everything else."

Awesome. $18 plus tip would buy a lot of ice cream. They walked out and got in the car together.

Once again, he knew he'd done the right thing. When she kissed him good night later, he thought it might even pay off this time.

44.

Another important mission began the next day.

"Sloan, do you need any help with paying off your student loans?" Preena stood beside his desk while Jake waited out of sight a few steps away.

When he didn't answer, she continued. "Because we know that you've recently hired a consultant. Normally the consultant would take the lead and ask you a few questions, but in this case I think you have some explaining to do."

The truth was that she was bluffing. They didn't know for certain that Sloan had anything to do with the bad review and complaint from the bank. It was Preena's idea to confront him, and if he truly seemed baffled, they'd move on. But it turned out her hunch was right. Instead of putting up a fight, he folded like a roving street vendor who finally accepted that no one was ever going to buy his giant stuffed panda.

"I don't know what you're—" he started to say, before slumping in his chair. "Alright, I guess it's pretty clear. But how did you figure it out?"

"It was simple," she explained. "We just hacked into your accounts, installed a tracking device on your car, and set up a war room down the hall to monitor all the leads."

"Wow. You guys are *good*." He almost looked respectful.

Preena rolled her eyes and Jake emerged from out of sight. "No, Sloan," he said. "This isn't a true-crime investigation that unfolds over the course of a fifteen-episode podcast. We just asked, 'Who would be such a jerk that they would go out of their way to do something like this?' And needless to say, there was only one answer."

"Oh." Now he looked disappointed.

"Seriously, man, I don't know what's wrong with you. No one here has it in for you, but you put a lot of energy into trying to make us hate you. What's the deal?"

Sloan looked down. "I just . . . I mean . . . it's really hard . . ." He stopped in midsentence.

"You just what?" Preena pressed.

They waited. He wasn't going to get off easy.

Somewhere in an alternate universe, a comet had just smashed into the sun. The people or aliens who lived on a nearby planet emerged from their homes, looking disoriented. All nuclear weapons were disarmed, and animals gained the ability to talk.

Because right here in the Brightside office, which would soon have Magnate's sign on the door, Sloan began to cry. And before long he wasn't just crying. Sloan was *sobbing*, head in hands, tears rolling down his cheeks.

The twelve-year-old girl inside of Jake wanted to say: *I literally can't even.* He started to put his hand on Sloan's shoulder, then pulled it away. Was he really going to comfort his mortal office enemy?

Stranger things have happened, he decided. *Some of them in the past month.*

He put his hand back and tried not to wince.

But also: *I literally can't even.*

"Sloan, you don't need to, uh, get so upset. I'll buy you a candy bar from the vending machine, as long as you promise not to ask for a refund. But you do need to tell us *why* you did this."

"It's a long story," he said with a sniff.

"We've got a long time," Preena replied, recovering from her shock and handing him a tissue.

It wasn't actually that long of a story. By the time Jake came back from the break room, Sloan had pulled it together and was ready to fully confess.

"So here's what happened," he told them. "I came in one morning and you'd just left to go on your big trip. Everything we do is logged on the server, so I pulled up the files you'd been working on. When I saw what you were doing, I got really mad."

Jake sat down across from him. "Mad?"

"Yes!" said Sloan. "At first I told myself I was mad that you were using the company's office to store your stuff, and working here on your own project through the night. Also, I think you ate the donut I'd been saving for breakfast. I saw a bunch of crumbs under your desk when I was poking around."

"Hm . . ." said Jake. "Maybe I did. There's this trick where you can use the microwave—but wait, let's get back to the point."

"Fair enough. I waited a few days and then put through that order and wrote the complaint. I used a fake email address so it couldn't be tracked back to me, or so I thought. Almost as soon as I did, I realized that my anger was misplaced. I wasn't mad at you—or if I was, I shouldn't have been. I was *envious*. I felt bad that I haven't been able to do something like this for myself."

He explained that a few years before, he'd bought into a network marketing program. The program promised to help its independent contractors "create financial freedom." The pathway to freedom seemed to be based entirely on purchasing large quantities of vitamins and supplements from the company, and then convincing other people to sign up. Sloan spent $800 on membership dues and supplies before giving up, and never made a single referral. He still had a stack of expired vitamin boxes in his garage that he had to look at every day.

"I knew there had to be a better way," Sloan told them, "but I felt discouraged about wasting my money, so I just didn't do anything. Then when I stumbled on what you were doing, and it actually seemed like it might work, it triggered me somehow. I felt bad after I called the bank. But I didn't know what to do at that point, so I just tried to ignore it. Maybe part of me wanted to get caught so we could have this conversation."

"So I'm really sorry, Jake," he concluded. "It was a dumb thing to do."

Jake didn't hesitate to agree, with one correction: it was a *really* dumb thing to do.

But he also kept listening. Sloan went on to say that he'd been under a lot of pressure, and it was affecting his whole life. He mentioned the title, Chief Asshole Officer, that Jake had secretly assigned to him.

"Wait, you know about that?" Jake asked.

"Of course. You guys aren't the only spies around here. And the truth is, I probably deserved it.

"Anyway," Sloan said, "I'm still mad, but now I'm mad at myself. I don't want to be stuck here forever, any more than either of you do. But what can I do? I don't have any skills in running my own business. I'm pretty sure I sold back all my textbooks to the college bookstore years ago. And I'm not sure there's any real service I could offer, unless anyone wants to hire me to complain about them online.

"Or maybe . . ." he started to say, drying his eyes. "You guys are both really good at this. Will you . . . teach me?"

Preena and Jake looked at each other, silently communicating that their minds were both exploding.

"We'll have to get back to you on that," Preena said.

———

The bad review came down later that afternoon. Student Loan Champion was no longer a scam. When Jake clicked the link in his news alert, it now went to a broken page.

The bank canceled the chargeback after Sloan called to confess. At first, Jake wasn't going to return his money, figuring that this hassle was worth at least $150. But when Maya encouraged him to take the high road, he decided to be charitable. In refunding the payment, he made things just as they were before the whole saga.

"You know," Jake said to Preena later, "in a weird way, it was worth it to see him come full circle like that. I have a feeling he won't be nearly as much of a jerk anymore. Or at least, not around us."

Preena had a slightly different view. "Oh, I thought it was worth it just to see him cry."

"Well, one thing's for sure. He owes me a lot more than a candy bar."

Sloan had made his confession at an interesting time: the very next day, Dirk Vanderpleitz would be visiting their office.

45.

The CEO of Magnate was a completely different person from what they'd expected. They were planning on meeting a weekend warrior type, one of those guys who got up at four a.m. to swim five miles before coming to work a twenty-five-hour day.

When a middle-aged accountant in a wrinkled, poorly fitting suit walked in, they thought he had the wrong address.

The accountant was carrying a sheaf of papers, most of which scattered to the ground when he tried to close the door behind him. He looked down at the papers as if he was surprised by the effects of gravity.

This was Dirk Vanderpleitz, the corporate titan who'd be deciding their future?

Even Sloan seemed a little thrown. Before his meltdown with Jake and Preena, he'd been preparing his best suck-up strategy. Between his confession and the vastly different figure that had just walked in, he'd need to reconsider the whole approach.

"Mr. Vanderpleitz?" Jan greeted him at the door, doing her best to disguise her surprise while stooping to pick up the papers.

"Indeed!" he said with an awkward smile. "And you must be . . . ah, sorry, who are you?"

"I'm Jan, the client services manager here. We've spoken on the phone a few times."

"Ah, of course! I remember very well," he said, with the confidence of someone who didn't remember at all.

Watching them interact, Jake suddenly had a theory. Sure, the disheveled appearance of Dirk Vanderpleitz seemed a little odd. *Unless he was secretly a robot*, transmitting information and receiving orders from headquarters in a hidden transmitter.

That's what it was about all this time.

It all made perfect sense, or at least it did for several seconds in his active imagination. The theory ran out of steam when Jake realized he could still be a robot even if he arrived in the form of the bodybuilder they expected. Also, those kinds of robots didn't really exist, as far as he knew.

They gathered in Jan's office and talked about the weather for a while. It was incredible, Sloan was saying, how sometimes it rains *even when it's sunny*. And did you realize, he went on, that the East Coast was often much colder than it was here in California . . .

Mr. Vanderpleitz cleared his throat. "Yes, that's fascinating. But I think it's best to get straight to the point. The truth is, I'm here on a mission from the board."

Aha. So he *was* a robot after all.

"We've had a look at the restructuring plan, and three of you will be staying on. Of the four of you, just one will be, ah, made redundant."

Made redundant. Most people would call that "fired," or if they were being more charitable, "laid off."

"Just like that? What about the assessment tool?" Preena asked.

"Yeah," added Sloan. "I thought everything was riding on that secret algorithm."

He shook his head. "We learned, ah, that the algorithm had some quirks. For example, it recommended eliminating our entire HR department, and since they do the hiring and firing, we weren't sure how to handle that. In the interest of saving time, we decided to move on manually."

Only one person was being let go. That seemed like good news, but who was it? Jake figured the odds were good that it would be him. It could also be Sloan—but given Sloan's ability to ingratiate himself (at least before the previous day's transformation), Jake didn't hold out much hope for his own survival.

Jan was ready to get on with it. "So what are we going to do, Dirk? Have a Rock-Paper-Scissors tournament to decide who's out?"

"Ah, that could be fun . . . but no, the board has already reviewed the data and made a decision. Does anyone object if I tell you all at once?"

No one objected. The unspoken consensus was: *Might as well see what we're dealing with.*

"Well . . ." He reviewed his papers one more time. "Preena, Sloan, and Jake . . . Magnate would love to move forward with you in our new combined operation. There might be another layoff in two months, but for now, you're safe. Jan . . . I'm sorry, but everyone agrees that we want fewer managers. We need to prioritize more of that crucial ROI we want everyone to focus on."

Wait, *Jan* was the one being let go? Preena and Jake couldn't believe it, and even Sloan looked a little unsettled. Jan herself was unreadable, at least judging by her initial reaction.

"Of course," he went on, "the board wants you to know that we really appreciate your service."

Jake knew he had to speak up again, but he didn't want to charge in directly. He channeled Clarence and tried an indirect approach. "Mr. Vanderpleitz, can I ask you a personal question?"

"Ah, well—"

He didn't wait for an answer. "I read in the Magnate newsletter that you've been married for a long time."

"Well, yes! Edna and I have been together for thirty-four years. We raised two boys, and a little girl who isn't so little now that she's—"

"That's great," Jake interrupted again, hoping he sounded confident without being too forceful. "It sounds like you have a wonderful family. When it comes to Edna, what's the ROI of your relationship?"

The CEO was puzzled. "Ah, well, I don't really think of relationships like that, Jake."

"Sure, but just stay with me for a moment. What about your boys and the not-so-little girl? What's the ROI of your three children?"

He considered the question for a moment. "I guess that's easier to answer. In financial terms, the ROI is highly negative. Even if you leave aside college tuition, raising a child all the way through teenage years is *expensive*."

"But worth it, right? Even though you're losing a lot of money?"

"I think I see your point." He smiled. "It's true that Edna and I didn't exactly analyze a spreadsheet before deciding to have each of them. But companies are different. Our whole motive is profit."

Jake stood his ground. "Respectfully, Mr. Vanderpleitz, I don't think it's *that* different. Not everything we do here, even as a company, can be measured so directly. This doesn't mean we need to lose money—not at all. Jan looking after her assistant who was sick was the right thing to do. But it's also an investment. You want to keep good people around, right? . . . That's a lot of what a good leader does, and Jan is a *great* leader."

Then Jake said something else that surprised everyone, including him.

"I can't accept Jan's departure. You have the right to make that decision, but if she goes, I go, too."

Wait, what? That part wasn't planned. It just seemed . . . like the right thing to do.

46.

This was what it came down to: Jake sitting outside the principal's office, waiting to be reprimanded for writing his term papers too quickly. They'd call his parents and suggest increased discipline at home. The only good thing to come out of it would be the extra time he'd have in study hall, which he strangely liked.

Except this principal's office was occupied by his employer, and the only study hall he'd have coming up would be a lot more time to go to yard sales.

A neutered version of Sloan sat in the corner, giving Jake a thumbs-up. Earlier he'd come over to offer his help with the follow-up work that was due for Rattlesnake Records. When he ran out to the coffee shop, he brought back lattes for both Jake and Preena, which they were reasonably certain weren't poisoned.

Jake checked the calendar to make sure it wasn't Opposite Day. It wasn't. It was just part of the new holiday that would forever be known as "weirdest week in the world."

Dirk Vanderpleitz had ended the meeting by asking him to step out. "I'm going to need to report to the board. Jan, ah, for now you're still in charge here . . . can you stay behind for a few minutes?"

Twenty minutes later, Jan came out while Dirk Vanderpleitz used her office to call Edna, or the board, or someone. She walked straight over to Jake. He started to say something, but she held up her hand in a signal to wait.

"Let's take a walk," she said. He got up and followed.

"So here's the thing," she said when they were in the clear. "I'm leaving Brightside. The decision is made and they won't take it back."

Damn. Well, a deal was a deal—he'd stand by his word.

"That really sucks, Jan. Like I said, you've been a great boss. And I wasn't kidding when I said I'd go if you did. I'm out."

She looked around again to make sure no one else was in earshot. "No, Jake, here's the thing. I don't *want* to stay. This is a better outcome for me, and it might be for you, too."

She went on to explain that she was ready for a change. Even before the assessment tool turned against her, she didn't have a good feeling about it. A while back she'd had some informal talks with a friend who worked at another agency. Those talks had accelerated, and the previous week she'd met two of the executives for lunch. She didn't have a formal offer yet, but the odds were good that it was just a matter of time.

"And this is why it's good for me," she told him. "I'd been planning to give my notice, but of course if I do that, I'm not eligible for much in the way of severance—"

"I see," he said, catching on. "But if they downsize you because of some ridiculous reason—"

"I'll get two months' salary as a cash payout the day I leave."

Two months' extra pay could go far. Even if she got the new job, she said, she wanted to take some time for herself. She and her partner had always wanted to visit Nepal. Now it seemed like they might get an all-expenses-paid trip, courtesy of Magnate.

"That's great, Jan," he said. "Way to pull a win out of such a bizarre situation!"

She shrugged. "I think I won the Rock-Paper-Scissors game without even playing."

Jake's thoughts shifted to his situation. "So . . . you're saying I shouldn't quit?"

"Not unless you want to!" Jan said. "In fact, I'm supposed to be out here trying to convince you to stay on to provide continuity during the transition. And since you've already said you were willing to walk away, my unofficial, nonboss advice is that now you have leverage. Dirk wants you around, so you should get something out of it, too."

Hm. Maybe it was time to actually put those negotiation lessons to work. Who knows, if he succeeded, maybe he could do some consultations . . .

His head was spinning. Before he could say anything else, they'd completed a loop around the building. He wanted to keep walking, but inside the door he could see Dirk Vanderpleitz frantically waving for him to return.

"Jake!" he called out. "I see you've been talking with Jan!" He wasn't known for subtlety.

"Just a minute, Mr. Vanderpleitz—I'll be right there." Jake stalled by pretending to go to the men's room.

47.

What did he want for himself, right now? He knew enough to know he should have a clear idea before the conversation began.

For a few minutes he tried to imagine what Clarence would do in this situation. He finally walked in and sat down at the table.

The CEO looked at him and began to make his offer.

"Jake, I respect your loyalty. It's an admirable quality. I also heard about your idea for Rattlesnake Records. Their team is saying that no one has ever been so straightforward with them before. That kind of spirit is exactly what we want to see! But Jan is moving on, and we still need you here. As part of the restructuring, we'd like you to stay on in a role with even more responsibility."

Don't speak too soon, Jake told himself.

"Thanks for the offer. I'm glad you have confidence in me." He kept his voice neutral as Dirk Vanderpleitz nodded.

"Indeed! So I guess I should say, congratulations are in order!" The CEO had a habit of hearing what he wanted to, regardless of whatever someone else was saying. "Ah, you do want the job, right?"

What would Clarence do?

He'd been asking himself that question all afternoon. All of a sudden, he had the answer: Clarence would look out for the people around him *and* find a way to improve the overall environment. If Jake could do that while also getting a raise, the weirdest day ever would turn into one of the best.

"Mr. Vanderpleitz, you were in the military, right? I think I read that in the newsletter, too."

"Yes, I was! Four years in the navy. Left as a lieutenant, and they paid my way through college. Bravo Zulu, best years of my life."

"That's great," Jake said. "I know someone . . . I mean, I knew someone"—thinking of Clarence in the past tense was always going to be hard—"who had been in the navy, maybe around the same time as you. I'm no expert, but I imagine that a lot of what you guys did was part of a pretty big operation."

"Huge! My aircraft carrier had more than four thousand people on it. We worked all three shifts."

"Incredible," Jake said, leading him on. "I guess it was really important that everything be done in a certain way."

"Yes, standardization mattered a lot. Everything had to be accounted for with no deviation."

"Makes sense. But does it matter as much for what we do here?"

"Absolutely. We're trying to make Magnate a market leader. We need a process that cuts out the inefficiencies. That's also something we learned in the navy," he added.

Jake made sure he fully listened before responding. "Well, here's what I think. I've never built a big business, so I couldn't say I know more than the people who have a lot of experience with that. But I also think that not everything can be so cookie-cutter. We need more of a human equation in some of our decisions, and that's something that Jan in particular was good at. She worked hard—and contributed to a lot of bottom-line ROI—but if someone needed help, she didn't hesitate to prioritize that relationship."

He looked out the window at the rest of the people in the office. "I know we need to measure things—really, I get it. I just want to make sure I'm part of an organization that doesn't miss the forest for the trees." It was all coming together. Maybe he'd even stick the landing in his third important speech of the week. "So it's important that I know my values are aligned with the new company's vision. I want to know that Preena's job is safe for the foreseeable future, and"—he couldn't believe he was saying this—"I want Sloan to stay on as well."

It really was the weirdest week ever.

Dirk Vanderpleitz almost lost his balance as he tried to casually lean back in his chair while considering a response. Jake pretended not to notice while he recovered.

"Alright, Jake," he finally said. "If we do all that, do I have your commitment that you'll stay around?"

Jake was silent for a few moments. It was all good news, and everything he'd said he wanted, but he didn't want to make a big commitment under pressure.

He'd come a long way in the past six weeks. He'd gained important skills and had the beginnings of a second income well underway. And though he hoped he wouldn't need to repeat the experience anytime soon, he'd gotten pretty good at living out of his car.

Whatever happened next, Jake was his own man now.

"Jake, are you still there?"

"Oh, sorry," he said. "Sometimes my thoughts get away from me."

He looked down at the floor and then back at his new boss, who instead of firing him—like he'd expected—had essentially offered him a promotion.

"Can I think about it?" he said in the end.

48.

The table at the coworking space was crammed with a wide range of coffee-related paraphernalia. There were two French presses, a handheld grinder, some sort of pour-over setup, and a full set of coffee and espresso cups.

Despite an abundance of equipment, its overseer was still in training mode. The pour-over had poured over onto the table. One of the four large bags of beans that accompanied the gear had spilled entirely onto the floor.

Adrian looked up sheepishly. "So . . . I'm not quite sure how to use all this stuff yet. But I thought it was important to try."

He'd taken on the role of Third Way barista and was discovering that it came with a learning curve.

Although the group had been together in various forms several times over the past two weeks, this was their first meeting to talk about their projects.

"Well, everyone," Adrian began as he handed out cups, "this is hard, and there's nothing I could say to make it easier. But I know that Clarence believed in this work, and I'm sure he would have wanted us to continue."

"Agreed," said Preena. "In a weird way, I'm even more motivated to work on my jewelry sales. I almost feel like he's watching us somehow, and I want him to be proud of what I've learned."

They sat in silence for a moment, feeling reflective.

Adrian finally spoke up. "Well, should we get started? It's been a while, and a lot has happened for several of us."

Jake had been sitting off to the side, watching the others. It was good to see Adrian stepping up as the group barista. It was one of the first things they'd talked about when they began to discuss how to resume the meetings on their own. He finally said something.

"For me, the past couple of weeks have been like nothing I've ever known. I hadn't even begun to download what happened in Ethiopia before . . . everything changed. I do have some project updates, but first I want to make sure you all had a chance to welcome another new visitor."

The visitor had arrived with Jake, and looked familiar to the rest of the group even though they'd never met before.

"Hi, everyone," said Zach. "I've heard so much about this group from Jake that I had to see it myself. And to be totally honest, I might need to make $1,000 of my own pretty soon."

Adrian reached over to shake his hand. "You're in the right spot! Alright, let's go to the phone lines, as they say."

Keisha was participating by video call from Phoenix and waved to them through the screen. "Hey, guys! I need some of that caffeine, because I'm heading to the night shift after this."

She told the group how the funeral had motivated her to move forward with the plan for her travel nurses program. She'd outlined a curriculum, partnered with a friend to start building the website, and given herself a deadline of forty-five days to launch.

"I've been sitting on my idea for too long," she said. "Looking around at everyone in the room for the service last week, I felt a sense of responsibility. I don't know if it will work, but I've promised to try. Hold me accountable!"

The group promised to check on her and provide support as she proceeded with her accelerated planning.

Preena spoke up next. "I don't have a big update, but I have a big idea. This is a little new, so if you hate it, it's okay . . ."

"Don't sell your idea short!" Jo exclaimed. "Just give it to us and we'll go from there."

Preena relaxed. "In short, the idea is that a lot more people need to know about this group. And not just the group, but the whole way of life that comes from it. I honestly feel so much better since I started earning money for myself, and I know most of you do, too."

Everyone nodded in agreement, and she went on. "I think Clarence shied away from that kind of thing because he didn't want to be the center of attention. But this work *deserves* wider attention. So what if we wrote up a description of the group, along with our bylaws, and made all the materials available to anyone else who wanted to host their own meetings?

"It would be decentralized," she continued. "Not about anyone holding power or profiting from it, but more about passing it on."

They all talked about how it would work. Someone would make a website, publish a list of best practices, provide a way for people to connect all across the country and beyond. It all seemed doable. And to make sure it remained decentralized, they'd already agreed that they would rotate the role of facilitator at their own meetings.

Then it got even better, when Celia spoke up. "What if we created a repository of ideas?"

"A repo . . . what?" Keisha asked from the video screen.

"A *repository*. Like, a big collection of ideas that anyone could use, or modify in their own way . . . or maybe even just to get them thinking." Celia looked around the room. "Who has ideas they haven't used? Something you've thought about doing, but discarded for some reason?"

Everyone in the room raised a hand, even Zach.

"I like it," said Adrian. "But there's one thing I'm stuck on:

Clarence always said that 99 percent of the work was in the execution of the idea. In other words, ideas on their own aren't worth much."

"Absolutely," Celia replied. "But the way I see it, if you don't have an idea to start with, you're stuck. So even if you borrow someone else's for a while, maybe that will lead you to one of your own."

That made sense. Then Jo suggested they adopt the idea in true Third Way fashion, and not wait to get started. "Why don't we make a list right now?" she proposed.

The group got to work. One person would suggest an idea, then someone else would jump in. Occasionally, they added to each other's comments, suggesting subtle tweaks or even wholesale changes. Preena got up to write them on the board in the front of the room.

- Don't just sell your own stuff—*offer to sell other people's stuff.* Lots of people don't want to mess around with online auctions. Go around and ask people what they want to get rid of. Handle it for them, and take a commission for yourself.

- Start an accountability service that sends you a text message every day asking if you're on track with your goals. If you answer yes, it sends a humorous photo to cheer you on. If you say no or just ignore it, it keeps badgering you with more messages until you make progress.

- Design an "inbox detox" service that unsubscribes you from unwanted mailings and allows you to de-

clare "email bankruptcy" by starting over whenever
you get overwhelmed.

- Make an app that automatically books a plane ticket
  for you based on destinations you select whenever the
  price drops to a particularly low level.

- Build a tool for farmers' market vendors to know the
  best place to set up, and what items are selling throughout the whole market.

- Propose a dating service for people who follow the
  Third Way model ("a new way of partnering up,"
  quipped Preena).

They kept going, and after twenty minutes they had close to fifty
ideas on the board. Not every idea was amazing, and not every one
would be a good fit for each person. But they were options, and
that was the whole point: *Ideas are for the taking. Pick one and get
to work.*

Between the two brothers, this time it was Zach who did all the
note-taking. He'd brought his laptop and was typing furiously.
When the brainstorming session ended, he took a picture of the
board to make sure he didn't miss anything. Jake looked over with
approval. He couldn't wait to see what Zach would come up with.

The group stayed late, fueled by the coffee and the surge of ideas.
There was something comforting about being together. They had
a new appreciation for the value of shared experiences.

"I don't know if any of you ever think like this," Celia said at one
point. "But I'm just so glad to be alive during this time in history.

It feels like there are an infinite number of things we could do. And more than ever, I sense how important it is to make the most of each day."

They all reflected on that for a few moments.

"That's exactly it," Preena said in the end. "There's a whole world of possibility out there. It's up to us to pay attention so we don't miss it."

49.

With the Brightside situation in flux, and the Maya crisis on the road to recovery, Jake took stock of his initial projects using the Third Way model.

He'd started with reselling—and reselling was good! The idea that he could make money whenever he needed, even if it wasn't a fortune, was powerful. The first few days of learning the ropes felt like he was competing on one of those reality TV shows where you have to start from nothing and find your way out. Except instead of being on an island with a hacksaw in search of a coconut, he'd made his escape from a looming financial crisis and temporary homelessness.

Still, as fun as reselling could be, it wasn't the final answer. As

Clarence had pointed out, it was a great start, but he wasn't really building a business, and he wasn't helping anyone other than himself.

His second project—once he'd abandoned the false start of being a negotiation consultant—was also good. He could see himself helping people find creative ways to repay their student loans for a while, maybe in the form of a few consultations per week.

But he had the sense that this also wasn't the final project he'd end up with. He'd started it up in a single weekend. What could he create if he had more time?

Jake didn't *need* to find a bigger project right away—Clarence had told him more than once that it's better to focus just on what's in front of you instead of searching for the meaning of life—but he'd grown a lot in the past two months, and he was ready for more.

Clarence's death motivated him to keep searching. He didn't want to settle for anything less than something that he'd be proud to show his mentor. So if he began with reselling and then moved to a small service business, what came next?

The inkling of an idea had been in the back of his mind, and he'd been thinking about it off and on since the funeral. The idea was far from being fully formed, yet a few persistent themes kept coming up.

Ethiopia. The meetings with Yonas, the villagers, and Eshe at the factory. The problems that Micah, one of the Third Way members, was having in sourcing a manufacturer for the exercise gear he wanted to sell.

There was some connection between all of them. Or maybe that was exactly it: there *needed* to be some means of connecting the people from one place with people in another.

Jake had grown up in a world where everyone was on the same big social networks. You could argue about politics with strangers, or you could keep to yourself, seeking out information and groups that supported your existing views. You could stalk your internet crush to see their fifth-grade photos and favorite inspirational quotes. Still, there were limits to these networks. Jake realized that he mostly used them to connect with the same people over and over, whenever he wasn't watching urgent videos of cats on vacuum cleaners. It wasn't until he went on the trip to Ethiopia that his eyes were opened to a world of new possibilities.

There should be some kind of online global village, specifically for everyone who's trying to pursue a Third Way project on their own.

He pictured a message board of some kind, where anyone who registered could post on two lists. One list would be "I'm looking for . . ." and the other would be "I can offer . . ."

It wasn't a matter of one group "rescuing" the other. People on both sides had struggles and advantages of their own. The problem, and therefore the opportunity he saw, was in finding a way to bring both sides together.

———

The next day, having slept on his idea and after spending most of the morning in full-on Brightside mode, he took a lunchtime break at the coffee shop across the street and wrote more notes. As best he could, he thought about how Clarence would have framed the conversation if they were meeting at the Lava Java.

"Alright, Jake," he imagined him saying. "What's the idea, exactly?"

It's a network to connect people around the world with different needs.

"People with needs . . . okay, but who, specifically? Is this for everyone?"

Jake had learned that lesson. Whatever he did next, it definitely wouldn't be for *everyone*.

No, it's for people like us—he'd tighten that part up later—*the ones who are trying to start these little moneymaking projects, but need help finding resources and connections.*

"Okay. You probably need to get more specific than that, but it's a start. What's the revenue model?"

If Clarence were really here, Jake thought, now would be the time where he'd lean back in his chair and pause. This was the critical question, also known as "How will you actually make money?"

On this point, he felt a little stuck . . . at least at first. That was why he hadn't done anything with the idea yet.

Part of him was tempted to defer the question, but he remembered the advice from back in the first group meeting: Don't skip the revenue model. Decide on this sooner, not later.

Preena had also said something memorable during one of their chats: "If you don't have a way to make money, you have a hobby, not a business." It was something she reminded herself as she built out her jewelry line.

As he thought about it more, an answer emerged: this would be a *membership site*. Participants would pay a monthly or annual fee to participate. In exchange, they'd get access to the network—and not just the network, but maybe a series of trainings. A weekly newsletter. A spotlight on different vendors that offered low minimum quantities to help members get started without breaking the bank. The project (and, hopefully, his profits) would be funded by those contributions.

This membership model worked well because he'd have predictable income. He remembered Clarence nudging him in the village when Ajani, the bread baker, stood up to tell his story. Thanks to a new agreement with the village school, Ajani knew he'd have a certain amount of orders to fill every week. This made it much easier for him to invest in his business and build up a savings fund. What did Clarence say then?

"Recurring income! This is so important, Jake."

Jake already knew how important recurring income was for bigger businesses. It was something they worked on a lot at Brightside. But in starting his own projects, he hadn't really considered how to apply such a model. Now he had his idea.

He started running numbers, estimating how much he'd earn based on projections of the number of members and the price he charged. Maybe there could be a tiered pricing structure, to make sure that lots of people could join. It also seemed like the kind of thing that would go over well as a crowdfunding campaign, at least once he had something to show for it.

Also, if he didn't want to focus on growth so much, he could build the membership base to a sustainable level, then focus his time on making the community better and better.

Clearly, he still had a lot to figure out—but he also had a solid vision. This had real potential. Whatever he did, he wanted to give back, *and* he wanted it to be profitable. Through Clarence and the Third Way group, he'd seen firsthand that the two goals were not mutually exclusive.

———

Exciting as it was, this idea was also a lot different from buying textbooks, where he could achieve results right away. He'd have to be more patient. Even so, he knew he'd follow the Third Way model in building it out. He'd bootstrap it, learning everything he needed to along the way, and getting an early version of it out the door as quickly as possible.

Just a few weeks before, the corporate consultant in him would have immediately started thinking about how to construct a pitch for investors. You couldn't do something like this on your own, right?

But now he knew it was possible. Or at least he thought it was worth trying. In the worst-case scenario, he'd spend a bunch of time learning more skills . . . which was hardly a huge loss. Besides, he thought about what Zach had been going through over at Buzzard. Clearly, the business model they were using was flawed. If their service was so great, why did they need investors to keep bailing them out? A truly helpful product could generate its own funding, and be better off because of it.

With bootstrapping as his core operational value, he'd make a plan. Time to get out those workflows again and start writing a bunch of lists.

He'd poll the Third Way group, of course. He had a feeling that they'd help sharpen the idea a lot further with just a few conversations.

He'd ask Maya (and maybe her family!) for advice. This was right up her alley.

He'd also ask Zach to be part of it somehow. Maybe a big part? Even though Jake didn't love the Titan way of doing business—and definitely not the Buzzard one—he knew that Zach's experience in that world could be helpful. He made a note to check with him.

Now that he thought about it, Liza would be going to Southeast Asia next summer. Assuming he stuck with the project, maybe there was a way she could get involved, perhaps meeting with potential vendors or new connections on her trip. It would be fun to work together on a different kind of project in this new phase of their lives.

And, of course, he didn't need to stop doing the student loan sessions while he was working on the new idea. He could build for the future while providing for himself in the meantime.

———

Now he just needed a name. What would he call it? Names had always been important to him. Student Loan Champion had worked so well because it was clear, descriptive, and memorable. So what would he call his network to link up different people around the world?

He started thinking more about what it would do. Then he made a list of words he associated with his idea: *community, connection, marketplace, relationship, knowledge,* and *value* were some of the first ones that came to mind.

A couple of early possibilities popped up:

> Global Doorstop—Because that was what he imagined it would be: a place where you could find someone to make designer scarves in India, or get advice on immigration to New Zealand
>
> Smaller World—Because that was what he was doing: making the world a little smaller by bringing people together

He knew they weren't quite right, but he also knew not to eliminate any idea in the brainstorming phase. There was something about both of them that he liked, and the goal was to extract whatever that thing was.

He wanted to bring the Ethiopian village to his front door. He wanted to connect people on both sides for mutual benefit. And since he couldn't fly over Ajani, Yonas, and the rest of the gang, he'd have to make it an experience that everyone with an internet connection could take part in.

That was when it hit him. He'd call it Virtual Village.

All of a sudden, he could picture the whole project. Maya was leading a workshop for the next couple of days, so his evenings were free. He'd start work on it that night, right after he got home from the office.

50.

From: Kevin Quan
To: All Staff
Buzz team:

We've been on a kick-ass journey together, and I hope you feel proud of all we've accomplished.

However, I'm afraid it's time we accepted some hard truths. Our efforts to raise more cash have fallen upon deaf ears. I'm sorry to confirm that it's time to close things down.

I've recently started meditating, and it's been helping me process the transition. I'd like to leave you with a quote from the Buddha:

"Where you are is what you have been. What you'll be is what you do now."

I hope this helps as you consider your next steps.

On a business note, HR asks that you please leave the premises by 4:00 p.m. A cleaning crew from the landlord is coming by tonight and we have to have everything out.

Failing forward,

Kevin

———

From: Kevin Quan

To: All Users

Fellow Buzzers,

Important communication alert! I wanted to give you a heads-up on an upcoming transition we'll be making here at Buzz HQ.

Though we fought as hard as we could, we just couldn't sustain the ongoing cash flow needs of our office, team, and liability insurance.

Therefore, we're going to announce a *strategic pause.* After today, you won't be receiving any more decision reports, and our referral program is ending.

I'm also sorry to inform you that BuzzBucks™ can no longer be used for redemption in the online store. You may want to hang on to them as a memento of our time together.

We know there will be questions about what is happening with your data. Rest assured we're taking every precaution. A political polling agency has made a request to purchase much of it, but don't worry. We'll only sell it to them if they promise not to misuse it.

Don't stop believing (hold on to that feeling),

Kevin Quan

From: Kevin Quan
To: Hilary Hodgkins
Can we talk about strategy for the shutdown? I think there's a way to turn it into a more positive story.

To: Kevin Quan
From: Hilary Hodgkins
{Auto-Response; Message Undeliverable}
The person you are trying to contact is no longer with the company. She's out of the office for the rest of her life. She's not coming back, ever.

For Buzzard queries, please contact anyone who still does any work around here.

It's been real!

For personal messages:

Hils13PhiBeta@usc.edu

FOR IMMEDIATE RELEASE
Buzzard Announces Strategic Pause in Operations

Emeryville, CA—The innovative company known as Buzzard Co. announced today that it would pause its operations to "reflect and regroup."

Despite being a frequent target of online bullying and attacks by hackers, the service was truly ahead of its time. Its decision-making algorithm was only just beginning to come online, but it served more than 250,000 users with targeted emails. Many of these users received valuable, personalized recommendations for skinny jeans, ketogenic protein shakes, and life coaching sessions.

The company's founder, CEO, COO, and newly appointed spokesperson wished to clarify that he is treating this as an opportunity for growth, definitely not a permanent failure. He also promised to look out for departing team members.

"Meditation has always been important to me," said Kevin Quan. "We're encouraging our employees to reflect on this transition and come to a place of radical acceptance."

A large supply of high-quality, 100 percent cotton T-shirts will be returned to investors.

Contact:

Kevin Quan

KQuanChangi97@robomail.com

———

From: Kevin Quan

To: Zach Aarons

I said you could take a few things with you, but who's that guy loading all the desks onto a truck?

———

Buzzard Founder Takes to Speaking Circuit

Harrington Post

—

In an exclusive interview, Buzzard Co. founder Kevin Quan calls himself a "reformed startup boss."

The company famously crashed and burned after failing to achieve any of its objectives, but this self-starter is already thinking ahead.

"These are the times that really test your soul," he said. "And it's been really interesting. By meditating just ten minutes a day with an app I installed on my phone, within a week I felt much better about the whole situation. I knew what my next calling was."

Quan said that he plans to share his story at an upcoming TEDx event, and then pivot to becoming a motivational speaker for young people interested in the world of startups.

He's also offered to serve as a mentor for up-and-coming tech company founders.

———

From: Kevin Quan

To: Mercedes Maven, Corporate Speaking Success

Hi! I was given your name by a referral at the Harrington Post. I'm currently transitioning from leading a major startup to pursuing a new career in speaking.

Though I'm already an accomplished speaker, even the pros can benefit from a coach. I'm ready to level up!

At your convenience, please advise on rates, first available opportunity to meet, etc.

In the meantime, I'm making a list of topics that I think

audiences will find compelling. Here are my top three contenders—

1. Get It Over With: The Power of Big Mistakes
2. Other People's Money: The Proven Path to Risk-Free Growth
3. Leadership Lessons from a Las Vegas Jail: A Memoir

I hope to hear from you soon!

Kevin Quan

———

From: Kevin Quan

To: Katlyn Everett, Valley News

Hey Katlyn,

Not sure if you've heard the news—I've decided to move on to a new chapter. Even though we didn't always see eye to eye, I hope we can still be friends. I've always admired your writing!

I was wondering if you'd like to meet for drinks?

51.

The following weekend, Jake returned to his jogging track. He'd been working out sporadically at the gym, but wanted to get back to a routine. The new apartment helped a lot. Unlike his temporary mobile residence, the new place came with a shower.

He'd forgotten his headphones, but found he didn't miss them today. He ran the first few laps, warming up, and paused to stretch before continuing. Then he took off. He wasn't planning to run for time, but something in his mind urged him onward.

This time it wasn't the image of an Olympic race that propelled him down the track. He ran because as long as he ran, he was moving. For a circular track, it was funny how far away you could get from where you started just by running around and around.

Time can play tricks on you, he thought as he finished his first mile at a fast pace. It felt like just yesterday that he started at Brightside. It seemed like a decade since he met Clarence.

The pace caught up to him in the second mile. Slowing down to an accelerated jog, he thought back on the events of the past two weeks.

He'd taken Dirk Vanderpleitz up on the offer. Three new national clients transferred in from Magnate during the merger, and the office was busy. Jake was enjoying the new role. He knew he didn't want to do it for the rest of his life, but that was okay. He'd take it one step at a time, and for now the job brought him stability and a regular paycheck.

Jan wrote to him from her private email address to say how glad she was that the situation worked out the way it did. She expected to receive a formal job offer soon. In the meantime, she and her partner were planning a fourteen-day trip to Nepal. ("Thanks, Magnate," she wrote.)

Sloan had done a complete 180-degree turn and transformed into a loyal apprentice, volunteering to do odd jobs and forwarding internet memes to the rest of the office. He kept asking Jake and Preena about "that group thing" they snuck off to every week. So far they'd been able to avoid inviting him, but the other day they decided to pass along Clarence's manifesto. Preena figured if he was going to keep bringing them free lattes, at least he should find some way to pay for them.

Of course, Jake's day job wasn't his only form of work. He'd been plugging away at Student Loan Champion, signing up a new client every day or two. It wasn't retirement money, but it was working. He noticed he was getting better at the intake interviews he did. He tried to personalize each follow-up report, and he set reminders to check in with his clients every week for three weeks, and then every month for a year.

He hadn't received any other negative reviews.

As with the day job, Jake wasn't sure that student loan consultations would be his long-term project. The more he learned about the Third Way model, the more ideas he came up with for other projects. But that, he realized, was another advantage of the model: *you're not necessarily making long-term decisions.* There was little risk in proceeding with his best idea at any given time. If he had a better one later, he could change his focus.

That was what led him to agree to stay on at Magnate. The whole point of his "night job" was to bring in extra money, not replace his paycheck—at least for now. He wanted to pay down as much of his debt as possible, all while increasing his monthly side income. If it got to the point where he had to make a choice, he could figure it out then.

Speaking of Preena, she was also making plans. They had gone out for drinks the day after everything went down at the office. "I've set a goal," she said then. "A year from now, I'll be in Bali, and it won't just be a short trip. Whether I'm able to go all in or if it's just a month-long sabbatical, one way or another I want to pursue my dreams."

"That's awesome!" Jake was genuinely excited for her.

"And I hope we can help each other, Jake."

"Help each other?" he asked. "Preena, you were the reason I met Clarence in the first place. You've helped a ton!"

Even with no one in the office watching over them, they decided it would be better not to talk too much about their off-hour gigs while they were there. Instead, they initiated a weekly meeting where they'd review task lists and keep each other accountable.

Meanwhile, the group continued to meet every Thursday. Adrian had emerged as a natural leader, but he felt strongly that whatever power came with such a role should be shared. They set up a schedule where active members could sign up for different roles that would change every four weeks.

On a whim, Jake had reached out to Romeo George to ask for a favor. He wanted George—which was the name he preferred, but Jake always added the first part in his head—to show Zach some more about the reselling process. At first George was wary, but they agreed to meet and ended up hitting it off. It helped when Zach tipped him off about some free furniture that would no longer be needed at Buzzard.

Zach had a theory that he could help George build a website and film an online course about his method. There were people in every major city—and even plenty of small towns—who could replicate his small empire of large appliances in their own areas. Zach and George had gone in on a partnership and would split the profits fifty-fifty.

As for Jake and Maya, his special operation had been a success. This weekend they were going hiking. The following weekend, he was finally going to meet her family. Of all the hard-fought accomplishments he'd achieved in the past two months, this felt like the most important.

Cruising along, Jake finished five of his six miles and slowed down to a recovery pace for the final stretch.

Sometimes in life, a strange thing happens: we get the chance to reinvent ourselves. Our new self has the ability to draw on the strengths and experiences of the old self, but without the constraints and limiting beliefs that held us back.

When this opportunity arrives, we have a choice to make. We can use it as a springboard to greater things. Dreams become goals, and goals become a series of checkpoints along the way. As we achieve the goals and approach the dreams, new dreams appear on the horizon.

Or, of course, we can let the opportunity pass us by. That's why it's a choice: take it or leave it. It doesn't force itself in.

It was just like Preena had said at the last meeting: "There's a whole world of possibility out there. It's up to us to pay attention so we don't miss it."

Jake wasn't going to miss it again. He walked back to the Mazda and drove off into the new life he had chosen to build.

Epilogue

—Sixty Days Later—

Jake walked in the door and put down his bags. "Anybody home?" He'd been away for a few days to meet with the East Coast office in Philadelphia.

"Perfect timing!" came a reply from the living room. "I just got in from work ten minutes ago."

They weren't exactly living together, but Maya had been staying over at his new place more—and he'd been staying over with her, too. Jake could tell that one of those defining-the-relationship conversations would be happening soon. And, he thought, this time he wasn't totally afraid of it.

They greeted each other and began catching up while he unpacked. She was in the midst of telling him about a new literacy program they were starting at work when she suddenly remembered something else.

"Hey, before I forget, I picked up your mail on the way upstairs. You got something that looks like it came from a lawyer."

Hm. Lawyers weren't known for sending friendly greetings out of the blue. Had he received another chargeback? Did Sloan go back to his old ways and decide to sue him?

Jake stopped unpacking and went over to the counter. When he saw the return address on the large envelope, he stopped worrying. Instead, he felt a rush of other emotions all at once.

The letter was from Clarence's lawyer.

It was fairly heavy for a letter, with two extra stamps affixed to the envelope. He held it in his hands for several minutes, thinking back. He remembered the village in Ethiopia, where he became an instant celebrity and gave out more high fives in one day than ever before. He remembered riding around with Clarence and Yonas in the Land Cruiser, staring in amazement at all the roving vendors. The whole time he was learning, he was also having the time of his life.

Then he remembered returning to California and seeing Clarence drive off for the last time. A week later he was looking out at a roomful of people, doing his best to honor his friend while promising to live for something. The memories were intense. Some of them, he sensed, would be with him for the rest of his life.

"Well?" Maya said, jolting him back to the present day. "Why don't you open it!"

He did so carefully, peeling back the envelope and revealing a letter, something that looked like a check, and an oversized coin. He started with the letter.

Dear Mr. Aarons,

We spoke on the phone and then met briefly at the funeral following the unfortunate death of my client Clarence Johnson. I appreciated your speech at the service. It's obvious that Mr. Johnson had a profound impact on your life, as he did for many others.

As part of the extensive preparations he made, my client entrusted me with a set of instructions that I have followed to the best of my ability. First, I am enclosing a modest payment with this correspondence. Mr. Johnson instructed me to wait several weeks, and then make a series of payments from his estate to anyone I determined was particularly important in his life.

As you can imagine, it's a long list, so it took a while— but I found my way to you. Mr. Johnson did not outline any conditions or requests for this gift, so you are free to use the funds however you see fit.

In addition to the payment, I was instructed to pass along a special coin, which is also enclosed.

Mr. Aarons, I'd like to once again express my condolences to you and your friends in the group. Life is indeed all too short.

Best regards,
David Wiezman, Esq.

He put down the letter and looked at the check. The total was $1,000, payable to Jake Aarons from the estate of Clarence L. Johnson. One thousand dollars—the same amount that Clarence had challenged him to come up with at their first meeting.

It was a final act of generosity, and maybe an unspoken assignment. This time, instead of earning $1,000 for himself, he had to determine the best use for an unexpected gift.

Jake knew right away what he'd do with the money. The name sprung to his mind: Eshe, Yonas's daughter, who was starting the bag-making business. Investing in Eshe would pay off more than any stock or bond. They'd kept in touch, and she would be launching her campaign soon.

He didn't need startup capital for his own projects. Besides, if he ever *was* in need of extra money . . . well, thanks to Clarence, now he knew where to get it. He'd found his money tree after all. But a thousand dollars could help Eshe in a much more significant way. She could hire another employee or purchase extra equipment. He'd make the donation on the first day of her fundraising campaign, in addition to a pledge of his own.

"We need to look out for each other," Clarence had said that day they were talking on the guesthouse porch. It was another statement that seemed simple at the time, but profoundly important later.

The oversized coin was still in the envelope.

Jake took it out and held it in his hand for a few moments before looking down. When at last he did, he saw that the front side bore an image of a coffee cup. *That's appropriate,* he thought. *At least as long as the coffee is fair trade and organic.*

He could tell from how it felt that the back contained some kind of inscription. Without turning it over, he already had a good idea of what it said. Still, when he finally allowed himself to look, his face broke into a big smile.

You can do more than you think.

Note from the Author

Thank you for reading *The Money Tree!*

I wrote this book to teach people a new way of thinking—one that will set them free from the burden of debt and empower them to have more control over their future.

If you know someone who's stuck, I hope you'll share it with them. A book like this will succeed only if enough readers talk about it. If you don't recommend it to people who might find it helpful, they might not ever hear about it on their own.

You can send them to MoneyTreeBook.com, their favorite bookstore, or any online retailer.

Or better yet, buy them a copy. They'll be able to repay you later . . .

To the buzz,

Chris Guillebeau

FROM *NEW YORK TIMES* BESTSELLING AUTHOR

CHRIS GUILLEBEAU

"Chris Guillebeau is a rare
combination of sage and adventurer."

—SUSAN CAIN, *New York Times* bestselling author of
Quiet: The Power of Introverts in a World That Can't Stop Talking

Available wherever books are sold